GET OUT OF YOUR WAY!

JARED JAMES

GET OUT OF
YOUR
WAY!

...AND FINALLY GET WHAT YOU WANT

YorkshirePublishing
www.yorkshirepublishing.com
Write Now.

Paperback: 978-1-949231-45-8
eBook: 978-1-949231-46-5

Get Out of YOUR Way!
Copyright © 2014 by Jared James.

Yorkshire Publishing
3207 South Norwood Avenue
Tulsa, Oklahoma 74135
www.YorkshirePublishing.com
918.394.2665

ACKNOWLEDGMENTS

LIKE ANYTHING THAT anyone does, there are always so many other people that are involved than just the one or few that get the credit, and my story is no different.

I want to thank first all of the people that have supported and followed me on social media, in our programs, and in any other way. It has been my privilege to grow and learn with so many of you.

To my mother, thank-you for sacrificing so much when I was a child and giving me the opportunity to succeed. I hope that I pay it back to you every day.

A HUGE thank-you to my family. Without my wife, I couldn't do any of what I do. Your support and partnership in helping to change people's lives go unnoticed too often but know that I appreciate you and thank God that I have you with me on this journey. We've been together since I was sixteen, and you have probably thought I was crazy at times with my ideas and dreams but you stuck with me long enough to start seeing some fruit.

To my two awesome boys, you guys not only changed my world but you also continue to change it every day. I could never have imagined loving two kids as much as I love you guys. One day when you guys are older and you see this, you may not know the journey that your mother and I went on to give you the opportunities that you have but know that we would do it all over again. Everything we do is for you two. You make us proud every day.

CONTENTS

11

12

INTRODUCTION

YOU DO MATTER

DID YOU KNOW that there are over seven billion people on this planet and only one of them has the ability to keep you from getting what you want? Yes, people have influence over you, but nobody can drive you crazy unless you give them the keys. It's about time that we realized just how much power we have to create the kind of lives and careers that we desire and take responsibility as the one person on this earth that determines what we do with what we were given.

Writing this book was a longer process than I expected it to be because I cared about it so much. I knew that I wanted to write about something that would help people to get from where they are to where they want to be. I wrote down several potential titles and topics and, at one point, even got about half way through with writing another book until I realized it wasn't the book that I was truly passionate about at this time.

Through my job as a professional speaker and trainer, I get the opportunity to interact with a lot of people and most of them at a time when they are focused on bettering themselves and their careers. One observation that I have made about many of the people that I talk to who aren't where they want to be is the reasons for why they aren't there.

Most commonly, I hear about the economy, their friends or family, their boss or company, or something else along these lines. What I don't hear enough of though is them taking responsibility for where they currently find themselves. Unless, of course, they are satisfied with where they are. We are much quicker to take credit when we like where we are than we are to take the blame when we don't. I call it the quarterback syndrome. Most NFL quarterbacks love the press conference that ensues following a big win but don't have much to say following a loss. It's a great way to find out who your true leaders are.

When you think about it, we are really just acting on our human nature when we blame others because it is natural to protect yourself. If someone tries to hit you in the ribs, you cover up, and if our current situation is a result of the economy or some other outside force, then it is out of our control and we don't have to feel bad about ourselves.

The problem with this thought process though is that if our current situation is the result of factors outside of our control, then we also have to conclude that we don't have the power to change anything. If it is your belief that you are powerless to change your circumstances and the life you will live, then you might as well just get into a coffin and wait! That is not the world that I choose to live in and neither should you.

I do want to be clear though that I am not saying that your surroundings, upbringing, and the economy don't have any influence over you and your ultimate destination. Of course they do. But there is a difference between influence and total control. Too many people are allowing the wrong things to control their lives and their businesses, and my hope is that this book will help them in breaking this pattern in their lives.

Before I was speaking at conferences and writing books, I had a very successful real estate career. I have been asked many times why I would leave a lucrative career in real estate where there was no travel required to do what I currently do. The answer to this question is simple: I believe in what I do and the principles I teach and truly believe that I can make more of a difference on this earth by motivating and training people on how to start leveraging themselves as an asset and not their own worst enemy.

When you finally grab hold of the truths that I will layout in this book, they can help to reshape your relationships, financial situation, and overall outlook of your existence. To me, that is a powerful matter that will affect your current or future kids' lives and others for generations to come.

If you are reading this book, you can probably think of someone in your life or a book you have read that resonates in your head to this day and has helped to shape the way you make decisions and go about your life. My hope is that this book will be one of those moments for you going forward.

I have found that in most cases, the issue is not that we don't know what to do to get better or create a better situation for ourselves but the issue is that we don't do what we know to do.

Think of it this way: if you wanted to lose weight five hundred years ago, what do you need to do? Diet and exercise. What about 250 years ago? Diet and exercise. What about yesterday? The answer is still diet and exercise, and yet, we are willing to purchase a belt that straps around our waist and jiggles all day and if we act now, we can get two of them for only $19.99! Why? Because, please, anything but diet and exercise! It's too difficult!

You see what I mean? It's not enough to know what to do if we can't motivate ourselves to follow through.

I believe that when we understand ourselves, the world makes a lot more sense.

WHAT IT TAKES TO BE GREAT

Too many of us are so busy trying to be great that we are never able to be good. You can't be great until you are good first, just like you can't get to the number two without starting at one first. When you look at the types of personalities that tend to do great things, they can be a little controlling at times and have difficulty delegating. They want everything to be perfect before they will put their seal of approval on just about anything.

The issue with this is that it is not how the world works. Did Apple wait until the iPhone was perfect before it was released on the open market? Nope. The iPhone eventually ended up as an amazing product because of its imperfections and the feedback from users who weren't happy.

You are never going to be perfect, and every day you spend waiting until everything is perfect is a another day that your competition is moving forward; even if at a snail's pace, at least, they are moving forward.

It's the old adage that every journey no matter how long or short begins the same way, with one step. You have to just go at some point.

Like most things, there are those that will read this and take it to the extreme. I am not saying that you don't work on yourself, your business, or your product to make it the best that you can before moving forward with an idea that you have. I am just saying that you can't wait until it is perfect due to your fear of failing. After all, if you never try, you can never fail right?

This book really focuses on you though and getting you to a place where you are ready to dominate your area or industry by getting out of your own way. For that to happen though, you cannot neglect yourself while following your ambition.

Too many of us have invested so much time mastering our talents and skills that we haven't spent enough time on the sustainable resources of things like our character.

I believe that you can measure a person's character in two ways: how they treat those that have absolutely no ability to benefit them and by who they are when nobody else is around. Your character will carry you at times when other people would crumble.

I can tell you from personal experience that you are not ready to go after any big dreams that might bring you more exposure and a greater following until you have spent the time necessary to strengthen your sustainable resources such as your character. I am not sure that I agree that notoriety simply amplifies who you always were, but it can definitely amplify the worst sides of you and your most hidden desires if you allow it to. True character is the only answer to the pressures that can come your way when you succeed at whatever you do.

I have had to learn too many times to count that my character wasn't where I thought it was, but I have responded every time with the vigor necessary to grow and learn and become the person that my kids believe that I am. That is a high standard to live up to, but I am dedicated to reaching it with each day of my life.

> "What lies behind us and what lies before us are tiny matters compared to what lies within us."
>
> —Henry Stanley Haskins

1

IF YOU HAVEN'T BEEN THROUGH HELL YET...JUST WAIT

I GET TO talk to and observe a lot of different people on a regular basis. Some are happy with where they are at and some are not, but one thing almost every single person has in common is an inner belief that he or she could be or should be further along in his or her life.

There are many reasons why people are not always exactly where they want to be, but almost everyone can agree that it is because of...(fill in the blank). It could be the economy, or your boss, or your children and their activities, or the big one that you have gone through.

I truly believe that as a society, we tend to focus on a very specific set of addicts while ignoring the ones that surround us every day. Think about it, when I just mentioned the word "addicts," your mind probably automatically focused on drug addicts or alcoholics or something like that.

Yet we are surrounded by other types of addicts all the time and, in most cases, are an addict ourselves. Whether you are addicted to your phone, to a person, to sex, or to something as ordinary as food, you are still an addict.

An addict, according to the *Webster's Dictionary*, is someone that devotes themselves to something habitually or obsessively. Are you devoted to your work or something else?

I think if you were to step back and do an honest assessment of your own life, you may find that you are a little too devoted to or obsessed with the opinions of other people. No? That is for another chapter though.

Right now, I want to focus on what I believe to be one of the greatest addictions that people face on a regular basis that continually holds them back, and that is their addiction to their own problems and troubled pasts.

THE GREATEST HUMAN ADDICTION IS NOT TO DRUGS OR ALCOHOL

When was the last time that you asked somebody about their life or their past and they didn't start with a diatribe about how "it wasn't always easy" and "they did the best they could"? It probably hasn't happened all that often because we as humans are addicted to our own problems, even if they aren't as bad as we thought they were.

This, in my humble opinion, is why so many people are depressed and feel schizophrenic half the time. They are constantly comparing their inner selves, the things they know about themselves that nobody else does, and their addiction to what's wrong with them instead of what's right with them to everyone else's highlight reel. The truth is, like most things, probably found somewhere in between. Most people are not as good as they appear to be, and you are probably nowhere near as bad as you see yourself.

You have to understand that I am writing this as a person who was raised by a single mother and can vividly remember my mother lying in the corner of our apartment crying because she didn't get a job because she was "over-qualified" while she was worrying about how to pay the rent and keep the lights on. I met my father when I was twelve years old and watched as the other man that was supposed to be the father figure in my life abused my mother, both physically and mentally. My family and I lived in six different states growing up, many times because my mother was trying to get away from this abusive man. Of my mother's three sons, I am the only one to graduate from high school on time without a GED. I am skipping a lot of details but my point is not to talk about our struggles growing up, but more importantly, to show you that I could if I wanted to.

I would actually bet that many of you reading this book that are connected with me in some way through Facebook or Twitter or something else don't even know that much about my past as it pertains to the overly negative stuff. I assure you that this is not an accident.

In fact, I would even go on to say that when I picture my childhood, my mind immediately goes to the happy times, because they are there. As I am writing this, I am reminiscing on my times with my best friend as a child, Liz, and how we used to ride our bikes together and share secrets.

Regardless of how you grew up, I promise you that you had good times and bad times, but whichever you decide to focus your mind on, you will find. In fact, by not deciding to focus on the good, your mind will automatically go to the bad because you are addicted to your own problems and it makes us feel better to have an excuse for where we are just in case we don't get what we are going after.

Just so you don't think I am inserting my opinion here alone, did you know that your body is actually addicted to negativity and being upset? It is true. When you get upset, endorphins are released into your bloodstream just like a drug. You literally crave more of it.

Just like a caffeine addict needs more coffee or a drug addict needs their drug of choice, our body has become addicted to the feelings that the endorphins release in our body when we focus on things that are negative.

This can be a real problem until you realize that you can crave success just as bad and become just as addicted to positivity, but you will never even get to that point as long as you allow your craving for negativity and problems to take root and stifle any chance that anything good had in your life. You must defeat your addiction to negativity before you can ever embrace your passion for anything worth embracing.

HOW DO YOU DEFEAT YOUR ADDICTION TO NEGATIVITY?

Be aware. Most experts will tell you that the first step in defeating anything is to be aware that there is something to be defeated in the first place. I am betting that many of you reading this book were not aware that endorphins were released into your bloodstream when you got angry, upset, or depressed. Now that you know it, own it and make the decision that this is not okay with you since it has no internal or external benefit to your life or career.

One of the things I do when I am trying to figure something out or am just thinking through a problem or someone else's problem is that I ask myself what the end game is. In other words, if I do this, then I am hoping for this to happen. Or if he or she does this and it works, then this will be the result. Sometimes something as simple as completing a series of actions in your head and seeing the result can help you determine which way to go and what to do.

It is amazing to me how many people make dumb decisions solely because they never made the effort to actually invest some time thinking things through. Hence, the line that a frustrated person will often say, "What were you thinking?" In some cases, you just weren't.

NOBODY CAN DRIVE YOU CRAZY UNLESS YOU GIVE THEM THE KEYS

It is one of the reasons why I don't get why people get so upset about what other people have said to them and end up getting into a war of words. What's the point? What's the end game? So you said something to try and degrade me, even though you don't matter to me. I call you on it and let you know that I know what you were doing, you don't matter to me and have a good life! Now what? If you truly didn't matter to me, why would I spend all that time arguing with you and allowing stress into my life for any longer than it deserved? It brings me back to my original question of "what's my end game?" If there is not going to be a possibility for a positive result, then I am most likely not going to waste my time and neither should you.

Remember, nobody can drive you crazy unless you give them the keys! I had a situation in the past where somebody that knew me called me up and brought to my attention a blog that was devoted to bashing me.

According to this blog, I was a terrible person out to get people and on and on. My friend was enraged and wanted to know what I wanted to do or what did I want him to do. I looked at the site, read it over, and responded by telling him that what I wanted him to do was go back to work and forget about it.

Well, he was outraged. "Shouldn't we do something?! This is ridiculous!" I replied, "Is anything they wrote true? Because if it isn't true and they don't even know me and I don't know them, I am not going to give them the keys to drive me crazy. Go back to work."

Some of you reading this book need to do this with people who are not unanimous bloggers, but in your case, they are a little closer to home. They might be friends, family members, or someone else, but you can't allow people that don't deserve the power in your life to continue to have so much control over you. That starts now.

Starve it. You kill an addiction the same way you kill anything—you starve it. Addictions live and grow the same way that anything does. Their appetite is fed by whatever is going to give them energy, and our continual thoughts and actions that support our addictions to our problems and negativity are not different.

We feed this addiction by the people we hang around and the content we digest. Haven't you ever noticed that negative and gossipy people like to hang around other negative and gossipy people? You aren't going to kill a plant by watering it and you aren't going to kill an addiction to negativity by hanging around other negative and self-pitying people. You have got to get away from them and surround yourself with people that make you feel awkward if you start on your "negative, I come from nothing, crap train."

When you swear like a sailor but you hang out with people who do the same, chances are you have been desensitized to your foul mouth. But if you were to walk into a church service and talk to the pastor or priest the same way, you would know pretty quickly that it wasn't acceptable.

This addiction to our own problems and negativity is the whole reason that shows like the *Housewives of just about everywhere* and others are able to exist. Let's face it. They aren't getting ratings because of their model example of what a good and loving marriage should look like. They get ratings because of their inner fighting and gossiping and the promoting of all the things that we secretly love but don't want to admit. You will not break your addiction without starving it, and this starts with taking a good, hard look at the content that you digest on a regular basis. There is a reason that the news industry has a saying "if it bleeds, it leads." Positive news doesn't sell, but unfortunately for you, negative beliefs and addictions don't promote you to where you want to be either.

Replace. Simply taking away something when you are addicted to a feeling won't permanently eliminate that addiction. No more than trying to eat better and saying that you are going to eliminate hot dogs from your diet, only to replace them with cheeseburgers. All you have done is eliminate one negative and replaced it with another negative while still being able to say that you "eliminated hot dogs from your diet."

If you truly want to eliminate this addiction to your own problems, you have to continually replace your focus on the positive things in your life and from your past.

For example, I mentioned before that now when I think about my childhood, I immediately go to the good things that happened when I was a kid but that took practice and repetition. When you focus on something continually, it becomes your reality.

Think of it this way: is it at all practical to believe that a man, the Son of God, died two thousand years ago, rose from the dead and forgave all of mankind's sins? That sounds pretty ridiculous, right? And yet, this is what I and billions of others believe today. Why? Because we have been programmed to believe this through reinforcement and repetition, so much so, that it has become a reality for us.

Maybe that doesn't hit home for you. Does it make any sense to get into a large piece of metal carrying thousands of gallons of gasoline thirty thousand feet into the air over oceans and mountains captained by a man or woman that you have never met and trust that your life is safe? It doesn't make any sense at all, but every time you get on a plane, you are saying that it does make sense and you are confident that you will be okay. Why? Because even though you may be a little uneasy, you know that thousands of flights take off every day and land with almost no problems, and you are more focused on the landings than you are with the crashes. If you were focused on the planes that have crashed, you would never get on that plane to begin with, and some of you don't.

Is it practical to believe that when I walk into a room and flip some little switch on the wall that electricity, which I can't see, is going to generate enough power to start a light bulb hanging from the center of the ceiling? No, it is not. But every time I flip the switch, I expect the light to go on. In fact, the real surprise is when it doesn't. Why?

That's because we have been conditioned to believe in the outcome even if it really doesn't make sense if we really thought about it.

Your focus determines how you act and what you believe. You have to decide what you are going to purposefully focus on based on the kind of results and people that you want in your life.

2

HAPPINESS IS OVERRATED

I THINK WE all can agree that our emotions play a powerful role in how we feel and act on a regular basis. And most of us if we were asked what we wanted would respond with something like "I just want to be happy" or "I just want my kids to be happy" or whatever it might be.

I actually have read an article about a particular celebrity, and it always seems to be the same right after they have gone through their third rehab stint or fourth divorce. Almost every article reads the same. "(insert name) is finally in a happy place in her or his life."

I am going to tell you that I believe this is a big mistake and is part of what leaves so many of us depressed and disappointed.

HAPPINESS IS OVERRATED! Happiness was never supposed to be the goal. It is an emotion that goes up and down and, in many cases, relies on outside forces that we have absolutely no control over. It is an emotion just like anger or anything else. Nobody chooses to get angry, right? People do things that make you angry. So why would you want to leave your "happiness" in the hands of factors that you can't control? Things happen all the time that don't make me happy. Are you any different?

Well maybe we should just "choose to be happy." That's one of my favorites. Just choose to be happy and you will be happy. As if you don't really know how you feel and can just fool yourself into believing that you are happy. Keep this up and all you will create is inner conflict which is another monster all by itself that we will discuss later. Eventually, your inner self is going to rise up and yell back at you, "McFly! I don't care what you say. I'm not happy!"

The next time I go to get on a flight that is taking me home after an event or a long road trip and all I want to do is see my family and the flight gets cancelled, I can tell you right now that I am not happy. No matter how much I can try to tell myself that I am still happy, I'm not! I'm annoyed. I'm disappointed. I'm a lot of different things, but at that moment, happy is not one of them no matter how much I try to choose to be happy about my flight being cancelled.

So what should we do? Should we lower our standards and just live a compromised life with an acceptance that we just aren't going to be happy? That is not what I am saying at all. What I am saying is that happiness was never the goal. It is an emotion that comes and goes, and yes, when you have it, it is great. I love being happy. I love it when my wife is happy. I love it when my kids are happy. There is almost nothing better, but I don't always have total control over our level of happiness.

You know what I can control though—my level of gratitude. That's right. No matter what is going on, whether my flight is cancelled or not, or you get a promotion or not, or you made a sale today or not, or whatever your thing is, you can always control your level of gratitude in any situation you face.

LIST THREE THINGS THAT YOU ARE GRATEFUL FOR

I regularly refer to gratitude as the gateway drug to happiness. While I can't control happiness, as explained above, I can always have available to myself three things that I am grateful for at any given time regardless of what I am going through.

This is important to remember the next time a major commission falls apart that you were counting on or your husband forgets to pick something up after work for you that you reminded him about earlier in the day. Yes, you might be angry or disappointed that he forgot, but aren't you grateful that you have someone to share your life with?

One person's list of their three things to be grateful for may be completely different than someone else's and that's okay. In fact, it's more than okay—it's proper.

In the example I used above, I mentioned that your spouse might have forgotten to run an errand for you, but at least, you have someone to share your life with. But you might be single and can't relate to that example. In your case, you might be grateful that you didn't tie yourself to the wrong person at a young age and were strong enough to hold out for the right person. You see how this works?

It's important that you understand the power of shifting your gratefulness as well. Think of it this way. If I am grateful for someone close to me and then I find out that they have been diagnosed with a terminal illness, does that now mean that this whole theory of gratefulness was a farce? Of course not, but you have to know how to shift your gratefulness.

Instead of being grateful that you get to come home to that person every day, you may now be grateful that you got to spend twenty years coming home to them and for everything they taught you along the way. Either way, you always have something to be grateful for!

Don't allow this life to beat you down because it's not going to change. Bad things are going to happen. People are going to let you down. Close relatives and friends are going to pass away. I can promise you that, and I can also promise you that you will not enjoy these life events. But I can also promise you that the world will go on, and the way you attack the time given to you on this earth is 100 percent up to you, but it is not going to pause while you figure it out. Figure out now how you will handle difficulty in your life because this is not the playground and you will not get a do over.

So what are three things that you are grateful for? Take a moment to figure it out. Write them down somewhere at first and put them in your pocket. Soon you won't need them written down, but you have to remind yourself of what you are grateful for until it becomes your natural inclination to think like this, in the same way that you have unconsciously trained yourself to think first of your pain and problems. It takes repetition to create a new patter of thinking.

DIFFERENCE BETWEEN FEELING AND KNOWING

Growing up attending church for years, I have seen first hand the difference between people that know something with their head and intellect and people that feel something. America is a society that over 90 percent of its population identify themselves as Christians, or followers of Christ, and yet, how many do you think actually live a life that resembles anything that would look like someone that was trying to emulate Christ in their daily life? I think we would agree that we could all have areas or have had moments where if our lives were broadcast on a reality show, there would be inconsistencies. No?

This principle is true in so many areas of our lives but especially so when considering gratefulness. There is a difference between knowing that being grateful can be a powerful force in your life and actually feeling and experiencing it.

If you are having trouble feeling grateful, a great exercise to do is to find people you are grateful for and tell them what they mean to you. Many times the expression you see on their faces goes a long way. Instantly, they are grateful that you took the time to express to them how you feel and experiencing the feeling of making someone else grateful for something you did can work wonders toward helping you actually feel and experience gratefulness and not just know what it is in your head.

GREAT PEOPLE AREN'T GREAT BECAUSE THEY HAVE THE BEST OF EVERYTHING, THEY ARE GREAT BECAUSE THEY MAKE THE BEST OF EVERYTHING

There is this tendency among people to constantly compare themselves to everyone else around them. I really can't blame people for doing it either because in some cases, it can give you a great gauge of where you stand in comparison to others around you in similar situations. But there is a danger in doing this as well.

I mentioned earlier that we fall into a trap when we compare our inner self to everyone else's highlight reel because that is where the problem starts.

For most of us, we see the world through a completely different set of lens than those around us. In many cases, when we see someone doing well, we make assumptions about them such as nothing but good things happen to them.

I have been a victim of this many times in my life. If I told you how many times I have been told that "everything I touch turns to gold" or that I was the "golden boy." As if any successes that I have had or things that I have helped to create in my life had anything to do with the flat out hustle I invested or tough decisions that I have had to make.

Nope. It was just that everything I touched turn to gold. C'mon! Really?! That's because we tend to focus on the results in other people's lives and the process in our own. The results are glamorous and fun, but the process is muddy and exhausting.

The truth is that the very successful aren't successful because they HAVE the best of everything. They are successful because they MAKE the best of everything.

IT'S TIME TO CHANGE THE LENS ON YOUR GLASSES

Too many of us are wasting our energy continually trying to change our circumstances and, in turn, change our lives, but that is a complete waste of time. You can't always change the situation that you find yourself in, but you can change the meaning that you associate with your situation.

This is a way to metaphorically change the lens on the glasses that you view your world through.

This is a principle that, if you get, can fundamentally change your world as much or more than anything else that I can teach you in person or that you will read in this book. Stop trying to change your situation, and instead, change the meaning that you associate with your situation.

A great example of this was a conversation that I had recently with one of our coaching students. To give you a little back ground, part of my job is to travel to various places and speak at events with varying numbers of attendees. In addition to the travel, I run a fairly large coaching company designed for sales people, but primarily real estate sales people.

So one of the coaching students in our program sent me an email explaining to me how she had just joined our program and absolutely loved it and couldn't wait to get started. She then went on to tell me how she was in a terrible financial situation—her husband had lost his job and she was pretty sure that they were going to lose their house that they have lived in for over twenty years and raised their children in.

She went even further to tell me how badly she needed money, but the problem was that every real estate transaction she had been involved in since January had been so difficult that every time she gets close to a transaction with a potential buyer or seller, she is so sure that it is going to be as difficult as the rest of them and something in her turns off and she wants nothing to do with these potential buyers and sellers.

This was a real problem and a great example of inner conflict; I need money which comes through transactions but I don't want to deal with the very people who create transactions.

It sounds crazy, but at least, she was being honest with me.

At first, when I got this email from her, I was going to do what I would usually do and send her some sort of solution by email. If I had done that, I am sure that she would have thanked me for responding and probably would have truly felt like her problem was solved, but I knew in my gut that an email response wasn't going to solve her problem.

Because of this, I decided to respond, and she was available to chat briefly the next day like I have done with other students at varying times. It is not usually required and is not technically a part of our program that I call people personally, but my goal of the program was to truly help people and that means that sometimes you have to take a different route to get to the solution that you want.

I got her on the phone the next day and asked her a few very simple questions. I asked her what the number one source of transaction was in her industry. She told me that it was referrals.

I then asked her if that in a normal relatively easy trans-action, is it true that just about any agent could handle that transaction? She responded and said, "Yes."

I then asked her if it was true that in a difficult transac-tion, she actually had more of an opportunity to create more referrals to her current client's friends and family because they would see how much effort she was putting in and be thankful that they were working with her to help them through such a difficult transition in their lives and would actually be more likely to refer her to more people because of the job that she did under such tough circumstances?

She responded by saying, "Yes. That makes sense."

So I said to her, "So isn't it true that you should actu-ally be praying for more difficult transactions since you need the money and referrals are the number one source of income in your industry?"

She paused for a moment on the phone and sounded completely baffled before telling me that she should be praying for difficult transactions.

Think about what I did with her. Did I lie to her? No. I simply changed the meaning that she associated to her current situation, which, in turn, changed the way she approached her career and attitude.

She sent me an email a couple of months later telling me how she had closed on our new transactions, had some money in the bank, and her whole mentality about her life and business had changed.

Now, that is the kind of turn around that I live for.

She couldn't immediately change her financial situation without robbing a bank, but she could change the mean-ing she assigned to her situation, which led to her financial situation changing anyway. Just like you can't choose to be happy but you can focus on what you are grateful for, which many times, leads to happiness in the end.

Along the same lines, I was at an event recently where I was the doing the keynote address to over one thousand attendees. It wasn't difficult to get my energy up for this address. In my industry, I have always found it easier to speak to five thousand people than fifty people.

For this particular event, I was contracted to not only do the keynote address but also to do a breakout session after as a follow-up for those interested. When I was done with my address, I was walking over to the breakout room with a guy that was a Facebook friend that I was meeting for the first time in person. As we entered the room where the break out was to take place, it was significantly smaller. In fact, it probably had about 150 seats, and my new friend was quick to get annoyed and tell me how terrible this was and nobody is going to fit in here. "What were they thinking?" he said in reference to the event organizers.

Now, I had a decision to make. Should I take part in his opinion about the room and join the complaint party that was going on. Everything that he said was true. No, I would not. Instead, I looked at him and told him how packed the room would be, standing room only, and that this would add to the energy and excitement level that the attendees would feel. I mentioned to him how I would have dreamed to be able to fill a 150-seat room only five short years ago.

I couldn't change the room, but I could change the meaning that I assigned to the situation I found myself in that I had no control over to change this late in the game.

Are you noticing a trend here? I hope so because life really isn't that complicated until we complicate it by not understanding how we were created to function.

Sooner or later, we have to do more than just read a book like this; we have to actually start implementing it's principles to see the results that we want in our life.

I'm no different than you. The moment I stop being intentional about my life, mediocrity will show up at my doorstep in a moment's notice willing and able to take over my entire thought life and patterns.

Protect yourself like you would for one of your children or a child that you love and care about. We are no good to anyone else if we don't take care of ourselves first and foremost.

My life is filled with all sorts of temptations, stresses, and struggles, and when I look back at the times that I have fallen short of the standards I have set for myself, it has happened because I stopped being intentional and allowed complacency to rear it's ugly head. Lesson learned. What say you?

3

WHAT'S YOUR STORY

IT IS NO great revelation that the old saying "sticks and stones may break my bones, but words will never hurt me" was a complete farce. Sticks and stones do hurt, no doubt, but they will be dealt with by a body that was created to heal itself. What I am more concerned with is the power that words have.

The most popular book of all time, the Bible, even broaches the subject. Proverbs 18:21 teaches us that "life and death are in the power of the tongue." That's a pretty strong statement regarding words that supposedly "will never hurt me."

Words have the power to tear down or build up a child's self-esteem. In about, the time it takes to watch the intro on the average commercial you can literally damage a human soul for life by telling a child that he or she is a loser and always will be. That's why some of you reading this are still so affected by what your father said to you when you were six years old.

If you aren't convinced of the power of words, then try walking into your local bank and saying out loud for everyone to get down and nobody will get hurt. Even if you don't possess a weapon, just the mere sentence will send shivers down the spines of anyone who happens to be making a deposit or withdrawing some cash at that particular moment.

So while it may not come as much of a surprise to you that words have enormous power, think "I have a dream!" or "Mr. Gorbachev, tear that wall down!"; what may surprise you is that for most of us, it is not someone else that we have to worry about bad mouthing us or tearing us down.

Let me ask you a very simple question. Who spends more time with you than you? Who talks to you more than you? Think about it. Everywhere YOU go, there YOU are.

I don't know about you, but I wouldn't want to spend a whole lot of time with anyone that didn't have a high regard for me. Don't you like to be around people that generally like you and speak positively to you and about you? Of course you do! Yet in many cases, we do not apply the same censor on our own words to our self that we do to other people.

If any one of your friends was struggling financially and came to you frustrated because they had a completely unproductive day and needed someone to talk to, what would your response to them be? I promise you that it would be different than your response to yourself.

If they asked, "How come I don't do what I am supposed to do?"

You would say, "It's okay, honey. Just keep trying and you will get there" or something like that.

But if you didn't do what you were supposed to throughout the day and had one of those conversations with yourself that we all have, it would go a little differently. You would ask yourself why you didn't do what you were supposed to do today, and your answer to yourself would be, "Because you're lazy and irresponsible!"

Wow. That's quite a different way than you would talk a friend, family member, or someone else that you loved.

So why is this important? It's important because we all have stories that we tell ourselves. Like I mentioned before, nobody talks to you more than you so we better start taking control of what we are speaking over ourselves because words have power!

Another word for story is a narrative and everyone has a narrative that they tell themselves that they believe to be true about themselves. Whether your narrative is true or not, it does not matter. What matters is whether your narrative is empowering you or holding you back. That is all that matters.

IS YOUR NARRATIVE AN EMPOWERING ONE

Your narrative can come from many different places—your environment, your upbringing, your parents, etc. But it should really only come from two places—what God says about you and what you believe about yourself.

Really, it should come down to what God says about you, but if you don't believe it, it won't become your narrative.

So what is your story?

Are you a single mom that will never be a top producer in your field because you can't devote the kind of hours that others can? Are you a single guy that can't commit to a good woman because you would be missing out on so much that the world has to offer? What is it?

I can tell you that neither of those stories seem to help you along the way to any kind of true success and are actually very limited in nature.

Did you know that when I was a kid, I saw abuse, poverty, and a lot of things that children aren't really meant to have to deal with? Of my mother's three kids, I am the only one that ever graduated high school, let alone college. To my brothers' credit, they both had the fight within them to wake up and go and get their GED. But my point is to illustrate how powerful your narrative can be.

I could have convinced myself that I just wasn't lucky enough to be born into a two-parent household with a loving mother and father who made a decent living. I should just be happy getting a job somewhere and having a somewhat stable life. I could have believed that high school and college weren't needed for someone like me because the type of job I was going to get just required that I worked hard, not what level of education I completed.

No, instead, I made the conscious decision to believe something else. I can remember as a kid writing back and forth with my Uncle MC while he was over in Desert Storm fighting as a member of the US Marine Corps and a light bulb went off in my head.

Haven't you ever had one of those "aha!" moments where something just made sense and it all seemed to come together? This was my moment. Don't let them pass without allowing them to impact you in the way that they were intended to.

I remember like it was yesterday, having this exact thought process go through my head. The marines have one of the greatest purposes on this earth—to defend their country and the freedoms we all enjoy every day. But they are not ready in their natural state to follow through on this purpose so they have to go to boot camp to prepare themselves for such a high calling. I also must have an amazing purpose on this earth that I have been lucky enough to go through life boot camp at such a young age.

Think about that for a moment. Rather than play the victim and decide that everything around me was terrible and not my fault and sulk, I decided to change the meaning of my situation which changed the story I told myself which changed how I felt and acted. I actually felt fortunate to go through what I went through because, to me, it meant that I had an amazing calling on this earth.

It's kind of like that old saying that God saves his toughest battles for his greatest soldiers. I chose to believe that. What do you believe?

I am well aware that some of you reading this right now just fell victim to exactly what I am talking about above. You read what I just wrote and you said to yourself, "Well, that's really nice, but Jared is just smarter than the average person and most kids wouldn't think like he did and turn their situation into a positive one like that."

Guess what you just did? You just did what you have done your whole life, and you created a narrative that is now going to hold you back. You told yourself that you were not as smart or aware as me and basically gave yourself a license to continue to struggle.

It's true that there are people reading this book who are smarter than me and there are people reading this book that are not as smart. Who cares! Whether you understood what I did at a young age or not, it doesn't matter. Are you going to continue to tell yourself stories that hold you back or are you going to take accountability for what you have now learned and change your narrative going forward. The past is where it belongs, and you don't live there any longer.

A story or narrative is so powerful that even political strategists and PR firms try to leverage it to their benefit. When political candidates are wrapped in a scandal during election season or are engaged in a debate where the narrative being discussed is mainly about their scandal, what do they try to do? They try to change the narrative by refocusing everyone's attention back on their track record as a peacekeeper and the job they have done on the economy. They know that if they can reshape the narrative and create a new story about what you think of when you think of them, then they have won.

The same holds true with the narrative that we create for ourselves and the story that we tell ourselves on a consistent basis in our own heads. If you can take anything good from a well-run campaign, it's how to change your story to something that helps you instead of something that holds you back.

WHAT IF IT'S TRUE THOUGH?

I want you to understand that a narrative or story doesn't have to be a lie for you to fall victim to it. Your narrative might be completely accurate and true. That is not the question though. The question is if it is empowering you or holding you back.

Some of you are holding onto resentment toward people in your past who have hurt you. You are angry at your mother who verbally abused you or didn't put you first. You are disappointed in your father who was absent in your youth and feel like they robbed you of a normal childhood.

The truth is that you are right. Whoever it is that you are upset with from your past, they probably were less than perfect, but again, the question is whether that belief if empowering you or holding you back. Change the meaning.

To be a strong person, you need to be able to give as much credit for the things people who have hurt you are responsible for as well.

For example, that absentee dad that you have held such resentment toward for years is also the very reason that you are as independent as you are to this day. He is the reason that you are as driven as you are, and that drive is what has carried you to your current successes. He is the reason that you are such a good parent to your children because you want them to experience what you never got the opportunity to experience growing up.

When you think like this, it makes it a lot easier for you to forgive other people and break the cycle of continual suffering on other people's behalf when they are probably not even thinking about you.

When you don't forgive others, it is like drinking poison and expecting someone else to die. It just doesn't work that way, but you also can't fool yourself into thinking that you have forgiven someone just because you decided to when you really haven't. You are much more able to forgive someone else when you spend just as much time focusing on what they are responsible for imparting into you as you do focusing on the negative stuff that they did to you.

BE HONEST WITH YOURSELF

I had a conversation just the other day after one of my events with a young lady that told me that she has struggled with her weight and an eating addiction her whole life. She explained to me how much she hates and how it makes her feel, and she just can't figure out why she has not been able to overcome her poor eating habits.

She said that she had tried everything. She's done every diet and most of them more than once, but nothing seemed to work for her.

Now, this is the time when I was supposed to tell her it's okay and she's going to be fine. She was expecting me to tell her to keep fighting, and eventually, she will overcome her weight issues if she just hung in there. That's what she was expecting me to say to her because that is what everyone else has said in response to her story up until now.

I couldn't do that though because I would have been feeding right into the very pattern that helped her to create the narrative that she believed which was that she was trying but it was just too difficult.

Instead, I told her to stop lying to herself and see the truth, which was that she was actually okay with her eating habits. She is not always happy with them, but she was okay with them.

Yes, there were times like weddings and other special events when she wished she was a little thinner, but overall, she had grown up in a family where just about everyone was over eaters. That's the model that she saw as normal. The very people that were fighting the fight with her to lose weight her whole life were the very ones that were overfeeding her as a kid and staying up late making plates of cookies and pies for the party the next day.

She needed her pattern disrupted in order to realize that she wasn't always happy with where she was but she was okay with it. Do you see the difference?

I told her that if she really wanted to change, she would. If I told her that she would be dead if she didn't change her eating habits by next week, do you think she would change her eating habits?

If I told you that your children were going to be taken away from you and you would never see them again if you didn't prospect for your business one hour a day every day this week, would you prospect for a minimum of one hour a day for the rest of the week? Of course you would! But if I just asked you to do it, you might do it for a day or two, but eventually, you would create a narrative about why you couldn't keep up with it. You would either explain to yourself how you had to service your current clients or that you had to attend a play at your kids' school or something else. That is what we do, but we have to learn to get out of our own way!

I told this young lady that until she came to grips with the fact that she was okay with where she was, she could never come to an honest conclusion that she was not okay with where she was because it was only in that place of clarity that she would finally see all the excuses and built-in barriers that she allowed in her life that were truly holding her back. You can't remove something if you don't acknowledge that it is there.

That's why people binge eat when nobody's around and don't do the things for their business that they should if nobody is around. They have created a life that is more about upholding an image of what think they should be rather than creating a life and business that actually reflects what and who they really are.

You can't ever change the narrative or story that you tell yourself until you solve this conflict.

YOUR NARRATIVE CHANGES THE WAY YOU ACT

Did you know that on May 5, 1954, nobody in history had ever run a mile in under four minutes? Thousands of years and billions of people had walked the earth but not one could break that supposed barrier.

But on May 6, 1954, Roger Bannister of England came along and ran, for the first time ever, a mile in under four minutes. That is not the point of what I would like to focus on though. As amazing as his accomplishment was, what others did afterward is what speaks to the power of a narrative on your results.

Within two years of Roger Bannister doing what nobody had ever done in history, no less than thirty-seven other runners did the exact same thing. So what happened?

I believe that for years, runners had told themselves that it wasn't possible, and if they were on pace to run a sub-four-minute mile, they would tell themselves to slow down because the narrative they had created was that it was impossible to keep up with that pace.

Once it had been broken though, the opportunity for a new narrative was created. Now, not only was it possible but it also had been done! Having a new narrative gave these runners something else to tell themselves, and it changed the way they acted. Now when they were on pace to break the four-minute mile, they didn't slow down and believed they could keep the pace.

What narrative are you telling yourself that you are having trouble changing because it doesn't seem possible or feasible or you haven't seen others do?

I'm not supposed to be keynoting major events with thousands of people at them when I am half the age of most speakers. I'm not supposed to be writing a book that thousands of people purchase and pass on to their friends. I'm not supposed to have a coaching program with thousands of people in it that pay to hear what I have to say. I'm just a poor kid from a broken home that grew up with everyone telling me to stop talking. What are you telling yourself that you are not supposed to be doing or are not capable of?

A single mom can make six figures and generate multiple streams of income, and an older man or woman can learn new tricks and change the way they do business in order to operate in a manner that the majority of consumers want to be communicated with.

Change your story and change your results.

FORGIVE YOURSELF

Some of you will read this chapter and still find yourselves unable to create a new narrative for your life because you simply are not able to forgive yourself for whatever it is that you have done in the past that has affected your life or the lives of those that you love so much.

Like anyone, I too have done things in my life that I look back on and have to ask, "Who the heck was that?!" I could never in a million years see myself making the same decision or decisions again, but nonetheless, I have made decisions that don't jive with who I consider myself to be.

It is important for you to understand that we are called human beings and not human doings for a reason. What you do does not always equal who you are at your core. Who you are and who God says that you are is what matters. What you decide to do and how you decide to act going forward is what matters.

The story that you determine for yourself will go along way in what kind of a human being that you will be and are.

4

MIND YOUR BUSINESS

THE BATTLEFIELD FOR your business, your life, and everything that you want is not necessarily where you might think it is. It is not found in how hard you are willing to work. Yes, hustle is a huge part of any success, but hustling in the wrong direction doesn't get you anywhere.

The battlefield is in your mind. Your body follows what your mind tells it to do. The way we were created, our mind determines what we want and what we are willing to do, and then it gives marching orders to the rest of our body to follow through with.

WHAT IS YOUR REALITY?

Part of my job requires me to travel to different places all over the world, and it is always interesting to say the least to see how different people's norms, values, and reality can be. In one area, it is completely normal for someone to go into the woods, kill a dear, and throw it in the back of their pickup truck, and in the next place I am at, if they even saw a hunting gun, they would be throwing up picket signs.

Have you ever encountered someone that is operating in a completely different reality than you? Have you ever gotten into an argument with someone and you could not understand why they weren't agreeing with you and did not even bother to change your argument. You just keep saying the same thing over and over again because you assume that they have to come down on your side of the issue in the end once they fully understand what you are saying.

What you are experiencing in this situation is someone that has a different reality than you.

Reality exists in the six inches between your ears, and it is just as real to one person as it is the next, no matter how different their realities are.

If I were to ask you a very simple question of "what color is the sky?" what would you say? Of course, you would say that the sky is blue because you are looking up at the sky and it is blue, right?

Think again.

The sky is not blue. There are atoms of nitrogen and oxygen that separate the sun's white light and it appears to be blue, but it is not blue. That is your reality though, and you would fight me to the death arguing that it is blue. How are you any different than these other people that you get so frustrated with when they don't agree with you?

Have you ever wondered why you can't tickle yourself? Some of you have had the experience of someone else tickling you to the point of peeing yourself, but for some odd reason, you can't tickle yourself. These are the kinds of things that keep me up.

In this way, I am very much like my buddy and fellow speaker Andy Andrews who once asked, "Hasn't anyone ever wondered why the glue doesn't stick to the inside of the glue bottle before you use it?"

The reason that you can't tickle yourself is because there is a portion of your brain called the cerebellum and its job is to perceive danger. That's why when somebody else tickles you, your body has a response, but when you tickle yourself, you have no reaction at all. It doesn't perceive danger from your own finger.

In fact, have you ever noticed that when somebody else tickles you, you've actually had goose bumps up and down your arm? Your body is actually responding the exact same as it would if you looked down and saw a tarantula on your arm—it's panic. To your brain, it is the exact same thing.

The real question is why does any of this matter? It matters because what you believe, what your reality is, ultimately creates what I call your worldview, and your worldview determines how you act and how much energy you are willing to put toward a desired outcome.

So is your worldview helping or hurting you? You are going to have to solve these kinds of questions in your head if you want to achieve just about anything in this world.

For example, I had the opportunity to speak to a group of real estate professionals recently, and I asked them if it was possible that I could bring each one of them individually into a separate room and then ask them how the market was and get a completely different response from each one of them? They all answered that it was not only possible, but probable.

If one of the attendees told me that the market was okay but there was still a record number of houses that were going to be released on their local market through shadow inventory lowering the values of traditional home sales, and 40 percent of all sales are effected by poor appraisals and lenders just came out and said they are about to tighten their standards to get a home loan and on and on.

If someone else in the same market said that mortgage rates were at an all-time low, the home affordability index was at an all-time high, over 30 percent of transactions in the last twelve months were all cash deals, meaning it is a great time for investors, and the *Wall Street Journal* just came out and declared the official end to the American housing bust and on and on,

The question is, "Who is right?"

Technically, they both are right, but again, the real question is which belief will empower you and which will hold you back because whatever you believe changes the way you act and the amount of energy that you are willing to put into a desired outcome.

If you have a belief that a certain number of transactions are going to fall apart, it's a numbers' game and that's just the way it is. I am telling you that there comes a point in every transaction where you tell yourself that story and something in you shuts off so you can focus on other stuff.

When you have a different belief and you know that there are more opportunities than ever before and people are able to communicate through social media and other channels in a way that wasn't previously possible, it also changes the way that you act within your job because your belief is different and the amount of energy you are willing to exert is heightened as a result.

You may be reading this and thinking that this is the classic glass half full or glass half empty argument and it may very well be. My greater point is on perspective though. Glass half full or half empty…you have water either way, right?!

So what will you do now? Will you say, "Okay. I am moving forward but this is going to take a while." I hope not.

It is always interesting to me when someone tells me how they dealt with something for so long and it had such a grip on them that when they finally decided to make a change, it took them six full years to change. That's complete nonsense. Change happens in an instant! It may take a little longer to see the results of your change, but the change inside of you happens in an instant. When you bake a meal, it may take a little bit to see the finished product, but you have the belief in knowing that the right ingredients are in the oven, and now, it's just a matter of time before they are finished cooking and you see the final product.

In a similar fashion, you may have struggled and danced around the issue for years. You "tried" over and over again, but then all of a sudden, something happened that affected you in a major way and you decided to finally change once and for all. The change happened in an instant!

This is why people struggle with eating healthier but never really make a change until they have their first heart attack. All of a sudden their "trying" days are over, and they just make a change because the reality of their mortality comes to the forefront and they are done messing around.

Someone else may have struggled with smoking for years and then their first little girl is born, and the reality that they want to be there to raise her hits them hard and, poof, they are done smoking.

What will it take for you to get serious about change? Will you need a major life-changing event or can you use this book as a wake up call to do what needs to be done to have the life you have always wanted and take control over the voice in your head and the words that you speak over yourself.

Start listening to that voice in your head. Is it empowering you or holding you back? It's that simple. If it is holding you back, it is time to read yourself a new book so to say. Get a new story.

THE WHITEBOARD

A couple of years ago, I used to run a large one-on-one coaching program all over North America. We had coaches everywhere and even more clients. It sounds so great but the truth was that I hated it. My whole life was being spent talking only to our coaches and event planners with no time left over to speak to the very people that I was supposed to be representing and helping.

During this time, I was on a tour in Canada, speaking at eight events in ten days, when I was approached by one of the attendees after I spoke at one of these events. He told me how much he enjoyed my presentation and asked me if I had a few minutes.

He then went on to tell me how for the past ten years he has made between $195,000 and $205,000, which sounded pretty good. Wouldn't you agree?

His frustration was not with the amount of money he was making. He was financially secure and come a long way. His frustration was with the fact that no matter how hard he worked or seemed to push year after year, his income didn't seem to change. He just didn't get it. He told me that no matter how hard he worked, at the end of the year, he was between the same $195,000 and $205,000 that he was making every year for ten years.

During this time, I still had the one-on-one coaching program going and even coached up to five people personally in order to stay relevant; then, he asked me if I would consider coaching him in an effort to help him break through this barrier he was encountering.

After I made the decision to work with him, I did what I would normally do and I looked at his patterns, systems, etc. and then asked him a very simple question.

I asked him if he had a whiteboard in his office that he used to keep track of the number of listings he had active and the number of buyers he had put under contract. He said that he did. What I found with him, just like with most people, was that his whiteboard was subconsciously being used as a motivator for him because when it got low and there weren't many transactions written on it, it kicked him into gear and told him that he needed to create more listings and buyer clients.

It is amazing how we can fool everyone else but ourselves because we know that there is a difference between going to work and actually "going to work." When that whiteboard of his got low, it was a trigger for him that he had to actually go to work and do things that he didn't want to do.

You can judge the level of success someone is going to have on this earth based on the number of awkward conversations they are willing to have.

When his whiteboard got low, he knew it was time to have some awkward conversations with people he didn't want to contact in order to set up the appointments he needed to create the new business that he desired.

Unfortunately, what was also happening though was that when his whiteboard was full, it was having the opposite affect. It was subconsciously telling him that he was okay and didn't need to work as hard because he had plenty of business in his pipeline.

I told him that you are doing $200,000 per year because you have a $200,000 whiteboard. It was really that simple. It was telling him when to kick into action when it was low and when to take a break when it was full, but it was in essence a $200,000 whiteboard.

As a result, I told him to do one of two things, either add four more whiteboards up on his wall or take it down completely. I needed to be able to push him fully every day without the distraction and limitations that the one whiteboard was bringing him. He decided to take it down.

Just to be clear, I am not anti-whiteboard. I actually think they can be great motivators in displaying to you and your office that business is happening, but you need to understand the negative effect that they can have as well once you start doing well.

I told him that for the next six months, I needed his full commitment. I needed him to agree to do absolutely everything that I requested of him—no questions asked no matter how ridiculous it sounded. If I asked him to get down in the grass and moo like a cow, I needed to know that he would do it.

He said that he would, with a smile on his face of course because it was a little bit of a ridiculous request.

Now that I got rid of that obstacle for him, I now needed to find out how to push him every single day. I told him that every single work day, he was going to work his tail off as if he was desperate and his children's eating depended on it. Would that change the way you would work? But I also told him that on his off days…guess what he was not going to do? I didn't want him working on non-work days because, as what I told him, he was driving his family nuts!

Even when you are not working, you are constantly checking your phone for emails and calls and anything else, and it is making them resent your job.

Not to mention, did you know that brain activity uses more glucose than any other activity that your body can do? You are actually working harder and becoming more fatigued when you are not working and just "checking on stuff" than when you are actually working. You have the right intentions; you are trying to be there for your clients, but in the end, you are failing them because you are never at your peak performance because you are wearing yourself down and never taking a true break.

Even a car needs to sit in the driveway over night and get an occasional tune up. You think you are any different?

I continued to tell him that I couldn't push him like I needed to if he didn't listen to and follow what I was telling him because his mind and body wouldn't be able to keep up.

After this conversation, I needed to find out what really motivated him. Most people think they are motivated by money but they are not. I had a conversation with a young guy recently and I asked him what he wanted in the next year. He told me that he wanted to make $250,000. I told him that he didn't and he responded that he did. This went on a few more times until I said to him, "Why? You want a bunch of paper with dead people on them?"

That is really what money is. It's not the money we are after, it's what we think the money can get us. Every goal or outcome is ultimately about the emotional feeling that we are after. So we want money because it will bring us security, and we can finally book a vacation for our family without worrying about the financial stress or we want respect among our peers or something else.

What do you really want? What emotional feeling are you trying to obtain?

Finally, once I found his source of motivation, I was now able to push him like I wanted to. Did you know that in months three and four of our coaching, he made more money than he had in any other twelve-month period in the last ten years?

Did you also know that the following January, he was named the number five agent in all of Canada and made over one million dollars in commissions?

What was the difference? Was it in him the whole time? Absolutely! But he was being limited by his limiting outcome that the whiteboard had helped to create for him. It told him when to turn on and shut off based on how full or empty it was and patterns don't lie. He had created $200,000 per year patterns, and the results followed until I was able to eliminate those limiting outcomes and create different patterns in his business.

You cannot put the ingredients in the oven for a pizza and expect lasagna to come out. You get what you deserve, good or bad, and you make the amount of money that you pattern yourself to make, but you have to get out of your own way in the area of your mind.

One of my favorite quotes that I keep near me at all times says, "Whoever said the sky is the limit didn't know there were footprints on the moon."

We are not limited by what surrounds us or the barriers that seem to conceal us. We are limited by our mind and the outcomes that we set for ourselves; that too often are what they are because of the stories that we believe about ourselves.

STOP SIGN, STOP SIGN, STOP SIGN!

I am fortunate to have two amazing young boys, who at the time I am writing this book, are six and four years old. My older son absolutely idolizes his daddy.

When I say idolizes, I mean it. The kid looks like my clone, but earlier this year, he cried himself to sleep because his eyes were a different color than mine. I have hazel eyes and he has brown. The other night, he went down stairs for a snack, opened up the door on the fridge, and proceeded to ask me what kind of a snack I would have had when I was six years old.

Now, you may be reading this and thinking, *Ahhhh... how cute.* But let me tell you, it's a lot of pressure!

One of the things that I do is I work out every other day and I run on the off days. Just for the record, I don't do this because I am trying to be some kind of a chiseled freak. I do it because I have two young boys, and I want to still be able to dominate them and their friends when they are in high school!

When I go running, many times, my boys will stretch with me, and while I run, they run around the house. It is not abnormal for me to come home and find them sweating more than I am.

Recently, my older son started begging me to allow him to go running with me. I told him that he couldn't because he wouldn't be able to run that far. There is a big difference between being an energetic child and running three and a half miles.

He kept pushing and wouldn't give up and was persistent in his questioning. We could learn a lot about sales from kids.

Finally, I gave in and said, "Fine. You can't run the full three and a half miles, but we will start by running to the end of our street." It's about three quarters of a mile and a good starting point.

So we stretched like usual, I showed him how to move his arms when running and off we went. We got about three quarters of the way up the road when he started panting and was out of breath. He told me, "Daddy. I can't go any further. I'm exhausted. I have to stop."

I tried to encourage him and tell him he could do it, but his body was telling him that he was finished.

Finally, the coach and trainer rose up in me and I looked at him and said, "Do you see the stop sign at the end of the street? We are just going to make it to the stop sign. Stop sign! Stop sign! Stop sign!"

I was trying to imprint the stop sign as an outcome in his mind because I knew that if I could, it would give marching orders to the rest of his body. Remember, the battle is not in the body, it's in the mind.

Now, keep in mind that the last quarter of the run is actually the most difficult part. It was all uphill and I was dealing with a six-year-old that wasn't used to running long distances. But, did we make it? Yes, we did.

And not a moment after we reached the stop sign did he drag himself over to the grass and throw himself on the ground and begin to tell me how he couldn't have gone another inch.

Could he have gone another inch? If a man jumped out of the bushes and started chasing us with a knife and wanted to stab us to death, could he have gone another inch? Of course, he could have! Somehow, his body would have found the strength to go as far as it needed to in order to escape the crazy man.

So why did he feel like he couldn't go another inch? Because that was the marching orders that his mind had created for his body to follow. His mind told his body that he was going to make it to the stop sign, and then he could stop and his body followed the orders given to it.

That is why many of you reading this book have had experiences where you have run a 5k and felt like you couldn't go an inch further and then three weeks later, you are running a 10k. You created a different outcome in your mind before you started.

Too many of us are limiting ourselves with limiting outcomes.

"Whoever said the sky is the limit didn't know that there were footprints on the moon." Makes a little more sense now, doesn't it?

THE ONLY THING WORSE THAN A LIMITING OUTCOME

In my mind, the only thing worse than a limiting outcome is to not have an outcome at all. I am well aware that many of the people that I speak to on a regular basis are so sick and tired of disappointing themselves by not hitting their goals or outcomes that they have finally just given up and have stopped creating goals altogether.

The problem with this is that you are working against how your body was created to function. Your mind gives marching orders to the rest of your body based on the outcome that it creates. So what happens when it has no out-come to communicate at all?

DON'T RUN UNTIL YOU ARE TIRED

A couple of years ago, I was on the road somewhere and it was my day to go for a run, but I was in a place where I wasn't sure how far three and a half miles was so I said something to myself that I knew when I said it was one of the dumbest thoughts I could possibly have. I said to myself, "Since you don't know how far three and a half miles is here, why don't you just run until you are as tired as you normally are when you run."

Sounds pretty innocent, right? Nope, it was completely stupid and I knew it.

For most people, just the fact that they stayed to their routine and ran even when they were outside of their ele-ment would have been a victory, but I knew that I was fool-ing myself, and yet, I still went forward with my idea.

So I went out and ran until I was as tired as I usually am when I run, and then I came back to my hotel. The next day, I got in my rental car to head back to the airport, and I decided that I wanted to see just how far I had run. So I turned on the odometer and went to where I had run the day before and then checked the gauge.

Do you want to guess how far I ran? I remind you that I usually go at least three to three and a half miles.

I looked over and saw that I had gone just over half a mile! Are you kidding me?! How could this be? I felt as tired as I usually did when I ran every other day. What happened?

What happened was that I was working against the way I was created and I knew it. Because I had no outcome to pass down to the rest of my body, it took control of the situation and decided that it was going to assign its own meaning to the exercise. Rather than the finish line I determined being the desired outcome, my body decided that simply being tired meant that I was done.

One of my favorite interviews was one that was done with Muhammad Ali when he was training to defend his heavyweight title. The interviewer asked him how many sit-ups and push-ups that he does in preparation for the big fight and his answer changed everything for me.

He said, "I don't count. No, that's not true. I don't count until it hurts because that's the only time it counts."

Do you know how much this has changed things for me? I used to tell myself when I was running or working out and felt tired, that I guess I had a good work out. I used to believe that when work got difficult I had finally done something meaningful. I now realize that when you start to feel that pain, that's not an indication that it's time to stop. That's an indication that everything I've done up until that point finally matters and to keep pushing because now it really matters. Those additional sit-ups are now going to show results in my stomach. The additional phone calls I make from this point on are going to reap amazing rewards if I stick to it.

I share this story so that you can see that we all are subject to these principles. It doesn't matter if you are a motivational speaker, someone reading this book or a professional athlete. If you don't give your mind an outcome to focus on and pass down to your body, your body will decide what it wants to do, and I promise you, it won't go as far as it could have. Your body is like an unmotivated hourly worker that looks for every opportunity that its boss is not watching so that it can slack off. Your body doesn't desire to push itself. That is your job both physically and mentally.

When I hear self-employed people tell me that they love not having a boss, I'm pretty sure an angel loses it's wings. You do have a boss! You are your boss, and some of you need to start being a little more bossy.

5

WHAT'S MY PURPOSE?

THIS IS EASILY one of the most common questions that I get from people. "What's my purpose?" or "How do I know what my purpose is?"

Before we get to that, let's solve something that I think you might be confusing up until now: your purpose is not your calling. They are two completely different things. Your purpose is whatever you "purpose" to do. Think of the phrase "I did that on purpose." It just means that you meant to do it. So your purpose on this earth is whatever you mean to or intentionally do, which is completely different to your calling on this earth, which is what you were put here to do.

Because people have been confusing these two for so long, it has led to billions of people feeling completely conflicted about their lives.

Did you know that your brain was created to pull from its external environment to support what it already believes? It's a defense mechanism that was intended to protect us.

That's why two different people can listen to the exact same president give the exact same speech and one uses what he said as a justification for why he is the anti-Christ and the other person that heard the exact same speech uses what he said as justification for why he is the second coming of Christ. Your brain is simply pulling from the exterior environment and assigning a meaning designed to support what it is that you already believe.

The issue with most of us is that this can actually work against us when you don't know what your purpose is. You come to an event and listen to a speaker like myself, and it motivates you and pulls you up. Then you read a book that you love and you take the information from it, and it pulls you to the left. Next, you watch a great movie, and it inspires you and pulls you to the right. Do you see where I am going?

You are constantly being pulled in several different directions following everyone else's purpose because you don't have any clarity on what your purpose truly is.

You were supposed to hear a guy like me and pull from it the information that was useful to implement to get you closer to your purpose. You were supposed to watch a great movie that left you inspired and take from it what you needed to get you closer to your purpose.

Without a true purpose for your life though, your brain can't do what it was created to do which only leaves you further down the road even more confused than when you started.

So the obvious question is, "How do I find my purpose and differentiate between my purpose and my calling?"

PURPOSE VS. CALLING

As mentioned above, there is a difference but I believe they can work together. For example, I believe that my calling on this earth is to help other people reach their full potential. I believe that I am gifted to be able to motivate, inspire, teach, and train others in a way that helps me to fulfill that calling.

Now, how I use those gifts is my purpose. I purpose to write books, give keynote speeches at events, write articles, and post relevant and uplifting content on social sites. In other words, I do all of this on purpose, and because I know what my calling is, I am able to decide what I should and shouldn't do every day.

If I am offered an opportunity that seems great, the filter that I use is whether it gets me closer to or helps me in my calling on this earth or not.

Using the example above about your brain being created to pull from the exterior environment to support what you already believe, I watch a movie and pull from it what I need to help me in my calling to help other people reach their full potential. I hear a great speaker or read a great book and pull from it what can help me fulfill my calling in some way.

A great example of this is something I experienced one day while writing this book. A year before that, I completely shut down the one-on-one coaching services that my company and even myself personally offered. I shut this part of my company down and went to a virtual coaching model because my life had become a daily pattern that consisted of me only having enough time to talk to my coaches and event coordinators that I was working with. I didn't have any extra time to talk to the very people that I was trying to help.

I needed to get away from this so I could leverage my time in a manner that allowed me to personally have more of an affect on people's lives. I may one day go back to a one-on-one coaching platform, but I will follow a different model and have somebody else running it that the coaches can answer to and bring their problems.

So that day, I was at an event and when I was done speaking, I was signing books and doing what you generally do after an event, and then a lady comes over to me and practically begs me to personally coach her.

She tells me that she will pay any amount and pay for the whole year up front. Seeing this, the people around me are astounded by this offer, but they are even more astounded when they hear me tell her that there is no amount of money that she can offer me that will change my mind on my coaching model at that moment.

Why did I tell her that I wouldn't do it regardless of the money? Because it didn't support my calling on this earth. If my calling was to make as much money as possible, then maybe I would have thought about it; although, I think there would be better ways even to do that.

In this example, though a new one-on-one coaching contract would have just taken up more of my time for an activity that does not get me closer to my calling, therefore it is not an activity that I am willing to purposefully do. Make sense?

Your calling is found in what you love. What are you good at? What gives you satisfaction? What do other people tell you that you are gifted at? And I am not talking about your mother telling you that you are a great singer. I am talking about other people. What is something that is greater than you and seems to be beyond your reach?

What would you need a little assistance from God to even come close to achieving? Your calling is found in that place. Everything else is just how you get there. You do on purpose everything that you know to do to get you closer to your ultimate calling on this earth. That is your purpose. Now, begin the search for your calling!

CONFUSION IS A GREAT PLACE TO BE

One of the six basic human needs is something called significance. We want to know that we matter and what we do matters. This is why people so badly want to know what they are here on this earth for. After all, it can't just be to grow up, fall in love, get married, have kids, and die, right? As if being a parent can't be an amazing calling. Try telling Billy Graham's mother that she was here for another purpose because I would argue that she has a pretty amazing legacy.

Having said this, you may find yourself searching for your meaning on this earth, and I have a little advice for you. Don't spend so much time searching that you miss all the opportunities that are right in front of you.

It wasn't my calling to sell kitchen knives when I was in college or to sell moving services at a relocation company after that, but I am glad that I had those jobs because I learned something from both of them that have helped me to this day and, ultimately, both were pivotal in getting me closer to my calling and meaning on this earth.

If your destiny is not 100 percent clear to you at the moment, then do what is in front of you and do it with excellence. Learn something from your current experiences but keep searching and be open to whatever your ultimate calling is on this earth even if it doesn't look like what you thought it would look like.

If you got a chance to talk to most people toward the end of their lives, they probably would have been surprised with what they ended up doing for the majority of their lives. I know that I never would have guessed that I would be labeled as a speaker, an author, or a coach. Shoot, I spent most of my childhood listening to people ask me if I was ever going to shut up! Now, I get paid to speak! Imagine that.

Regardless of how unlikely my outcome has been, I still made it a point to excel at everything that I was a part of while still always looking out for my bigger picture.

It reminds me of the old saying that the harder you work, the luckier you get. Luck happens to those that are prepared.

So prepare yourself! Work hard, have faith, and always have your eye toward what you are naturally talented at and how to get closer to doing what you have a passion for. Just because you aren't where you want to be yet doesn't mean that you are not on your way.

When I take my family on vacation later this year, we are going to have to get on a flight to get us to our resort, maybe even a connection along the way, but I will enjoy that ride because I know the outcome of the flights. It's easier to enjoy the journey when you know you are heading toward good things, but you still have to get on the plane. Don't be so focused on your calling that you miss the flights along the way that were put in your path to help get you there.

DON'T TRY TO BE SOMEONE ELSE

Another common mistake that I see people make when trying to fulfill their desire to find their significance in this world is to try and be someone else, and believe it or not, I get it.

One of the greatest ways to get what someone else has is to model the behaviors and pattern they followed to get it. But what if what they have isn't for you or you just weren't created to do the same thing.

I get more emails and messages than I care to mention from people that want to be a professional speaker. So much so that at some point, I will probably start an academy or training course designed for people that think it is for them, but it's not for everybody.

Too many people want to be a professional speaker for the wrong reasons. They think it will make them significant and important in the eyes of others without ever really questioning whether it is a gift that they possess or not.

Playing a professional sport or being a professional comedian is a gift that some have, and so is professional speaking. It takes more than just having a good personality. What amazes me is how many people who want to teach others have never really accomplished anything in their own lives that is of significance that they could pass on to others. Why would anyone listen to someone on how to climb Mount Everest when they have never climbed a mountain?

In the same way, why would anyone listen to someone about growing their sales numbers when they have never been a top producer themselves or had some sort of relative experience?

It also takes the ability to communicate your message in a way that moves people to the point of action, which is not easy.

My point is that if you are not an inspiring person that has the ability to motivate others in your daily life, then you can't expect this gift to manifest itself out of the blue just because you finally got on stage in front of people. Some are created to do this and some are not, and that is okay.

The ultimate goal of anything you do with your life is to serve, not to be served. The more fame you achieve was never intended to fill your ego more; it was supposed to be an even greater platform to use your influence to serve even more people in a greater way. When you think about your life calling deep down, you know that you are just trying to fulfill a void with attention from others; you may want to go back to the drawing board and not allow yourself to be self-deceived.

This applies to anything you choose to do with your life and career. Don't pick something just because you like what you see in someone else if the talents and skills that are required don't really fit your general makeup as a person.

We tend to focus on the highlights of others careers while ignoring the difficulties that can come with them. So you may see me on stage and greeting people afterward and all that come with that, but you don't see the countless hours spent in airports, on planes, and in hotel rooms when I would rather be home with my family. But something about my makeup allows me to deal with that lifestyle in a different way than many others would.

At the same time, I look at what others do on a regular basis, and I don't know how they do it. I was just created in a different way with a different calling on my life. Be honest with yourself so you don't waste valuable years of your life and countless dollars chasing something you were never meant for, whatever that may be.

In the end, why try to be someone else? They already exist, and you are never going to be able to portray them like they portray themselves just like nobody can portray you like you portray yourself.

You can take a trip to Las Vegas and go to see one of the many Michael Jackson impersonators. They will be entertaining, but in the end, everyone knows that they are not the real Michael Jackson. It is not what they were meant to be.

I had an organization that was hiring me to speak. They asked me if it was okay for them to film my keynote and make it publicly available to their followers to watch afterward. They were worried because one of the other speakers at the event had given them specific instructions that they were not to film him under any circumstances because he was afraid that other speakers might steal his content.

My feeling was that he was right that other speakers might. If you are out there and you want to steal other people's content, which is wrong, and present it at your events as if it were yours, you can try. But here's the catch. It might go over okay, but you will never be able to play the role as good as the original. In the end, you have made the decision to be a Michael Jackson impersonator instead of going after your true calling.

COMFORT IS YOUR ENEMY

People come up with so many different reasons for why they don't have what they want, and many of them are probably true. But I truly believe that one of the greatest obstacles to a great life is having a good life.

It's the "just enough" mentality. I'm doing okay, and there are so many others who are worse off. This kind of thinking will never allow you to reach your peak potential. You weren't put on this earth to experience a good life. You were placed here to experience abundance in all areas of your life. Don't be afraid to take calculated risks and chances along the way to create the life that you have always dreamed of. It's not like you are going to get a second shot at this thing.

This is the same mindset that allows you to live paycheck to paycheck because if you have enough money to pay the bills, then you are good. Well, good was never the goal; great was the goal!

That means different things to different people, but what does greatness look like for you? Have you settled in your business, in your relationships, with your health, or even spiritually?

There are times when we need to rest to gear up for the next battle or journey, but if you are stuck in a rest pattern, then you might want to reassess your situation. Some of the best advice I ever got was that comfort is your enemy.

Think about that for a moment. Comfort is your enemy. It's such a quick but powerful sentence that applies to just about anything that you do. We don't get results at the gym unless we experience pain. We don't get results in our business unless we do the things that others don't want to do. We don't grow personally without taking part in a certain number of awkward conversations. Comfort is your enemy.

There are, of course, exceptions and times that you need to experience comfort for a time, but don't lose sight of the larger principle. When I start to get too comfortable in my life, I start to worry because I am probably not building anything.

God saves his greatest battles for his best soldiers. If you are never in a battle, you have to start to wonder why you're riding the pine, so to say, in the game life.

So figure out what you are good at and learn to enjoy feeling uncomfortable because comfort is your enemy.

It is much better to blaze the trail designed for you than it is to visit the ones created by Lewis and Clark as a tourist. The tourist mindset will not ever allow you to build anything of significance or create a life worth being passionate about.

6

WHY MOST PEOPLE
DON'T HIT THEIR GOALS

IF YOU'VE COME this far, it means that you have some interest in what I am saying and for that, I thank you. I really can't cover the topic of goals too early in the book because too many of you would shut down the moment I even uttered the word "goals."

That is why for most of the book so far I have disguised them as "outcomes."

The majority of the people reading this book have experienced the disappointment of not hitting their financial goals, relationship goals, or wasting time on a failed diet. Did you start out saying, "Watch how bad I screw this up!" Of course not, but alas, it still happened.

What I am focused on is not that you have failed though, but more importantly, why did you fail? In this chapter, we will discuss that very topic. Why do most goals fail and how do we change that going forward.

MISGUIDED GOALS

The unfortunate truth for many people is that the goals that they set for themselves are not even motivated by what they truly want. This is obviously a recipe for disaster.

An example of this would be a young girl who has been asked to be in a friend's wedding party. She is all excited about it, and when she goes to the fitting for the dresses that she and the other girls are to wear for the big day, she all of a sudden doesn't feel so good anymore.

In fact, she even starts to feel like she doesn't look as good as the other girls do in the same dress and starts to believe that she is going to be compared to the other girls by the attendees of the wedding, and she doesn't like how this comparison is going to work out for her.

As a result of what she feels other people are going to think about her, she decides that she needs to lose weight.

Now, does she want to lose weight because of how she feels about herself or does she want to lose weight because of how she perceives other people are going to think about her?

The truth is that she might actually need to lose weight, but her motivation for why she wanted to do it is all wrong. The motivating factor of the wedding is going to come and go, and the question is whether she will feel the same way once the wedding is over or whatever event replaces it that temporarily brings back the same feelings to her.

This is why this same girl in many cases can be found sitting on her couch in gym clothes eating buffalo wings post-wedding and thinking to herself, *I really didn't want it that bad!* Once the event that spurred her insecure feelings was over, the motivation that came with it ended as well.

By the way, don't underestimate motivation. I used to get really upset when somebody would call me a motivation speaker. I would think to myself, *I do more than that! I teach life-changing principles!*

But motivation is a part of almost every success that you have had in your life. If the principles I teach are the metaphoric car, then motivation is the gas and what good is the most beautiful car in the world if it has no gas? In the same way, what good are your principles and strategies if you don't have the motivation to carry them through?

In the case of the girl above, she didn't have the motivation because her reason for wanting to lose weight wasn't about her to begin with. It was about what she perceived others would think about her.

So the first step in any goal is to make sure that it is real to you, no matter how crazy it sounds.

How do you make sure it is real to you?

NEGATIVE CONSEQUENCES

The best way to know if a goal is real to you or not is to come up with the negative consequences of not reaching that goal.

When my mother was raising me and my two brothers and had to make a certain amount of money to provide for us, what would this have looked like for her?

It would probably go something like this: *If I don't make enough money, I won't be able to pay the rent and we will be homeless. I also won't be able to buy the things for my kids that other kids have, and they might feel like they are less than the other kids.*

Those are real negative consequences, and you can bet were absolutely real to her. They meant something to her.

Now, here is the really cool thing about negative consequences. Have you ever noticed that music has the power to bring you back to the time when that song came out or was playing at a memorable time for you? If I were to play a song from your college days or whenever is meaningful to you, you would be back at that place in your head. It would be as if you were with those same friends, during that same time, at the same location.

This happened to me. I was in a sports bar in Pittsburgh where I was speaking the next day. While I was in the bar, the song "Poison" came on from Bel Biv Devoe. Without even recognizing it, I was bobbing my head and mouthing every single word and thinking about the people that I used to hang out with while this song played twenty years ago.

Music is powerful.

But here is my greater point. Just like music has the power to bring you back, negative consequences have the exact same power to bring you back to your original motivation.

When my mother set her goals for the year in order to provide for me and my two brothers and three weeks down the road, she didn't feel like doing what it would take to reach those goals, she could think of the negative consequences of not following through. *Me and my boys will be homeless, and they are going to feel like they are less than the other children at school. I'm motivated again!*

Nobody sets a goal and isn't motivated to carry it through at that original moment. The problem is down the road when it gets tough. That's when negative consequences come into play to bring you back to original motivation.

I use this in my own life. Because I have two young boys, I have a goal to stay fit, and as a result, I work out every other day and run on the off days. This keeps me exercising seven days a week.

What are my negative consequences? If I don't stay in shape, I won't be able to dominate them when they are in high school. Just thinking of that makes me motivated again. That may sound crazy to you, but I didn't set it for you. It's real to me.

DIFFICULTY IS A GOOD THING

At a certain point of time, many of you have experienced giving up on your goals when things have gone rough. You might not have made the conscious decision to give up, but you just started to gradually let them fade until you didn't think of them anymore.

In other words, you didn't say, "I'm going to stop going to the gym." You just started going twice a week instead of your normal four times, and then you were busy when you were supposed to go and it got down to once a week. And before you know it, you haven't been to the gym in six months.

This is actually how the gyms make their money. They couldn't possibly have room for all of the people that have memberships to work out at their facilities, but they are banking on this thought process from you to take affect.

So let's put the power of the "change the meaning" principle to action for you.

One of my favorite interviews was that of Muhammad Ali when he was training to defend his title belt. The lady interviewer asked him how many push-ups and sit-ups does he do in preparation to defend his title.

He responded by saying that he didn't count. Then he paused, thought for a second and responded, "I'm not really sure because I don't count until it hurts. That's the only time that it really counts anyway."

Wow! You have no idea how much that line has changed my life. I don't count until it hurts because that's the only time it counts. Do you have any idea how often I play that quote through my head when I'm working out and want to stop? When I am half way through my workout and I'm in pain and want to stop, I can finally tell myself a new narrative. "It finally counts!" When I'm running and want to stop because I am dead tired. "It finally counts!" When I am making difficult calls for my business or when you are prospecting and you don't like it very much. "It finally counts!"

The meaning most of us have learned to assign to pain or difficulty is to stop, but I created a new meaning, which was to stop when I reached my outcome. That was the whole point of the stop sign story with my son. I was trying to teach him a greater life long principle that being tired didn't mean he was done. He was done when he reached the outcome that he desired.

YOU HAVE TO LOVE THE RESULTS MORE THAN YOU HATE THE PAIN IT TAKES TO GET THERE

Negative consequences are an amazing way to really gauge how bad you really want something. If after coming up with your negative consequences, you are dissuaded from going after the goal you have set; then don't even waste your time trying. You are better off investing your time and energy on something else that really matters to you.

You have to love the result more than you hate the pain it takes to get there. There is a pendulum affect that occurs with every goal that we set.

One side is weighted down by the result that we want and the other is weighted down by what it takes to get it, and in the end, one of the sides is going to win. You have to love the potential result you are after more than you hate the pain it takes to get there.

When I wrote above about working out and running so that I could still compete with and dominate my kids in sports when they reached high school, that is going to require a lot from me.

I live in the northeastern region of the United States which means that our winters are extremely cold, and because I want to put my kids to bed at night, I am probably going to have to do the majority of my running late at night after they go to bed in the frigid cold over frigid ice and snow sometimes, breathing in air that is sometimes so cold it makes you want to throw up. That is what it is actually going to take, but in the end, I love the result more than I hate the pain it takes to get there.

THE DIFFERENCE BETWEEN INTEREST AND COMMITMENT

Too many people are going to work every day with the mindset of creating a job instead of building a career. When your purpose is to create a job, you are destined to always have just enough that you need to survive. You are destined to not be able to break through the barriers that seem to be holding you back. You are destined to be mediocre.

After all, you have probably seen before that the word JOB really stands for "just over broke." Some have decided that it's okay, but it shouldn't be for you. The very fact that you are investing the time to read a book like this means that you are by nature not a mediocre person and are willing to put in the extra effort that it takes to be more than average. Average-minded people don't read books like this. They read nothing but tabloids and self-serving magazines about how dysfunctional other people are.

When people are interested in something, they will get to it when their schedule allows and it is convenient, but when you are committed to something, you will not accept anything other than the desired result.

Your goals do not deserve your interest; they deserve your undivided commitment or they don't deserve anything at all.

You can't just commit to your job though. Committed people share a characteristic of commitment in most areas of their lives. If reading this book wakes you up a little bit and you decide to commit to your career while still only making a lack luster effort in the areas of your health, your family, and your spiritual life, it is only a matter of time before you find yourself lacking commitment to your career all over again.

That is because there are characteristics that have to be exercised for them to function but they can't only be exercised in the areas that you react emotionally to. If you don't believe this to be true, then try and be a good friend to one person and a terrible one to everyone else or a good parent to one of your kids and a lousy parent to the rest of your children. It doesn't work any more than trying to be a committed person in one area of your life without practicing this trait in other areas at the same time. If you are a good parent, you are a good parent to all of your kids, and if you are a committed person, then you are committed in all areas of your life.

Too many of us have walked through life with a wishbone mentality hoping things would work out and "wishing upon a star" when what we really needed was to drop the wishbone and get a backbone.

A backbone allows you to stand up to whatever you need to face and take chances and risks. Calculated risks but risks nonetheless.

So which are you when it comes to your career and the life you want to live? Is life happening to you or are you creating the life that you want? If you aren't actively investing the time and work required to create the life that you want, you will almost certainly invest your time and work helping to build up the life and career of someone else. That is fine for a while, but at some point, something in you has to step up and take the reigns. You don't get a second chance in life, but you do get as many tries while you are here as you choose to take. So step up to the plate and take a swing. You might strike out but, at least, you are a player. Players get paid while fans pay to watch. Which are you?

Failure is not an outcome unless you let it become an option. Failure is only ever an outcome if you stop. If you don't stop, failure is nothing more than a part of your process.

7

STATE OF MIND

ALL OF US find ourselves in different states of mind from one moment to the next. Our state of mind is usually defined by saying that it is your mood or outlook at the moment, and it is just as often described as being temporary. Our state of mind can change from one moment to the next depending on a lot of different factors from who we are surrounded by, what kind of music we are listening to, or even what kind of weather decided to show up for the day.

This can be dangerous though and here's why. Did you know that the top 100 sales people in the world all have one thing in common as a reason for their success? What they all have in common is the ability to control or the ability to manage their own state of mind.

Now before you read this and start to tell yourself that you are not in sales, I would argue that you are. I believe that everyone is in sales. Whether you sell real estate, shoes, insurance, or something else or whether you work in a corporation as an employee or manager or even if you are a stay at home mom or dad. Every day, all day, you are selling someone something.

Some of you are selling yourself on the idea of getting up and going to the gym, while others are selling their children on the concept of brushing their teeth and getting their shoes on so they don't miss the bus. So you see, we are all in sales in one form or another and are compensated in some form or manner as a result. Some collect commission checks while others experience less stressful mornings because their kids decided to buy what they were selling and got themselves ready in a timely manner.

You are always in some state of mind (mood or outlook), but the question is whether it's a good one or not and do you have any control over which one you find yourself in from one moment to the next?

HOW DO YOU START YOUR DAY?

What does it mean to wake up on the wrong side of the bed? Is it a good thing or a bad thing? The better question is for any of you that live with someone else, is it a good thing or a bad thing for them when you wake up on the wrong side of the bed? You know that it's true that when you wake up on the wrong side of the bed, it is not enough for you to be miserable. You'll be damned if anyone around you is going to be happy!

In other words, waking up "on the wrong side of the bed" means that your current mood or state of mind is not in a good place, and yet, the ability to control your own state of mind is a common characteristic of some of the most successful people in the world. I guess that we have a problem.

So what should you do?

My first question would be, "How do you start your day?" Regardless of what side of the bed you wake up on, how are you going to start your day?

Are you going to roll over and check your emails, most of them spam anyway; look at your social networks; or get a cup of coffee and just make it through the day? I hope not.

I start my day the exact same way every single day regardless of where I am or what I have on the agenda for that day, and I recommend that you do the same. For the first thirty minutes of every single day, I pray, read, immerse myself in good content, and watch good, uplifting videos. I did it yesterday, I did it today, and I will do it tomorrow all over again.

Why? Because they allow me to put myself in the state of mind that I need to be in to get the most out of my day and be more productive. Haven't you ever wake up ready to go and, for some reason, you get more done in the next six hours than you usually do in six days? Or on the flip side, you look outside and see that it's a cloudy day, and oddly enough, you just don't feel that productive all of a sudden?

State of mind is the number one reason for our success, and we are allowing things like the weather to determine how productive we are going to be for the day. How ridiculous is that?!

So how do you start your day? Haven't you ever watched the movie *Rocky* and wanted to kick someone's tail after it was over? The movies we watch and especially the music we listen to all help to create the state of mind that we experience.

The problem is that most of us know instinctively that we need to be in a good state of mind, but because we never know how to create it naturally, we fake it knowing that we have a responsibility to the people around us to be in a good state of mind.

Think about it. You could be at work exhausted, day dreaming about lying on your couch that night and zoning out with a bowl of ice cream. If on the way home you stop at the grocery store for some milk and bread, it doesn't matter how tired you are; if you hear someone call out your name in the store, you are going to turn around and say "HEY!!!" in the highest pitch of voices.

Seven percent of communication is verbal, and they say that the higher pitch your voice goes, the more you are lying. When you responded with "HEY!!!" what you were really doing was trying to figure out who you were talking to, but you responded in this upbeat manner because you knew that if it was a friend or past or current client, then you owed to them to be in a good state of mind whether you really were or not.

The danger in this is that we create so much artificial state of mind, known as faking it, that we eventually get worn down from all the acting. And who see this worst of us on a regular basis? Our family and closest friends. We get so tired of acting all day that by the time we get home, we feel like we finally don't have to act any more and the very people who mean the most to us end up experiencing the greatest divide in terms of our relationships with them.

We fix this by learning to manage our state of mind.

You can do this by starting your day the same way, but in many cases in the beginning, you may have to actually go through your thirty-minute morning routine several times a day until you learn a new pattern. There are some days that I have to repeat my routine from the morning again in the afternoon especially if I am speaking somewhere in the afternoon because I have a responsibility to be in my best state of mind when I get up in front of them, just like you have the responsibility to be in your best state of mind for the people around you as well.

We are more productive when we are in a good state of mind, and in the end, more people want to be around us as a result. Very successful people are not very successful because they are able to get more done in a shorter amount of time. They are very successful because they have more people working on their behalf.

With all the new marketing techniques available to us in today's world, don't you find a little interesting that the number one form of marketing still remains to be word of mouth? People work with people they want to be around and make them feel good. Period.

If you want to experience the benefits of people genuinely wanting to be around you, with the added benefit of referrals in your business, learn to control your state of mind.

State of mind is not only controlled by the videos you watch, the articles you read, and the music you listen to. It is also mainly controlled by the questions that you ask yourself on a regular basis.

THE QUESTIONS YOU ASK YOURSELF

In the first chapter of this book, I wrote about your story, which is what you tell yourself about yourself and your situation. In some cases, the story that you tell yourself is used as an excuse for why you aren't where you want to be, and in other cases, some of you use your story as a catapult to push yourself forward.

Either way, I made the point that nobody talks to you more than you, so you should be careful about how you talk to yourself because words do have power. For this reason, it is important that you pay attention to the types of questions that you ask yourself. Do you ask condemning questions that are meant to accuse yourself or do you ask yourself solution-oriented questions?

It matters because the questions that you ask yourself help create your state of mind. For any of you that have ever been on a diet, or better put a failed diet, you have probably experienced a situation where you have woke up with the complete intention of eating well, and before you know it, lunch time arrives and you fall off the wagon because cheesecake was offered up. Believe me, I know how you feel. I have felt the powerful Jedi-like draw of the great and powerful cheesecake as well.

When you have completed your meal and you are sitting down in a quiet moment of reflection, this is where the first wrong question is asked. You begin to question yourself and say, "Why did I eat so much lunch and why did I have that cheesecake at the end when I wasn't even hungry anymore?" Now if anyone else had asked you this question about themselves, you would be obliged to be much more caring and gentle with their feelings than you are with your own because when you ask yourself this same question, your mind kicks back an answer to yourself that sounds something like, "Because you're a fat pig that can't control yourself!"

Wow! Didn't that make you feel good? How's your state of mind doing now? Forget about production. You are just trying to figure out how you can skip dinner without anybody knowing.

The problem wasn't the cheesecake though. The problem was the question you asked yourself in response. Instead of asking an accusatory question like why did I eat so much, try asking a solution-oriented question like, "What do I have to do next time to eat better?" When you do this, your mind was created to come up with a solution such as "I'll eat a salad before I go places to curb my appetite" or "I'll take smaller portions next time," which gives you hope for the future instead of guilt for the past.

You can either leverage your state of mind to help you get more done in a day and feel better about what you do or you can allow it to constantly work against you, leaving you in a place where you always feel like you are swimming up stream trying to overcome your emotional state.

State of mind can't be faked without it leading to frustration, but it can be real and empowering when you put effort to manage it.

8

BUSYNESS VS. BUSINESS

THIS WORLD HAS so many traps set for you if you let yourself fall victim. One of them is the ideal of being busy. Some of us have learned to equate busyness with productivity and even importance.

We have really bought into the idea that the more busy we are and the more difficult we are to get a hold of, the more important that we must be. I am not proud to say that there was a time in my life when I bought into this way of thinking as well. The ironic part is that it was probably the point in my life when I was more broke than at any other time in my adult existence.

We have become such an ADD society that we cannot even say attention-deficit disorder anymore! We use mere letters to name the condition even! As you can guess, this is not a very good thing for our level of productivity.

I dare you to watch a commercial and take a look at how many different cuts there are to different screens in just sixty seconds. They know that we can't pay attention, so they are almost forced to do it.

This lends itself to us buying into even more lies that satisfy our appetite for busyness.

For example, many of you reading this book probably think that you are great at multi-tasking. Am I right?

Did you know that when you smoke marijuana, your IQ drops by about five points? Did you know that when you multi-task, your IQ drops by about fifteen points! It's even greater in men. Men were made to focus; we compartmentalize.

It's why I love talking to men when they are in the audience because I know that they are actually paying attention to what I am saying! Most of the ladies in my audience are paying attention, and then they are figuring out if they like my shoes, and then they are thinking about their shopping list for later, and then they are paying attention again! Ladies, kindly correct me if I'm wrong.

A couple had been into an argument before they headed to a friend's house for dinner. By the time they get in the car, the husband is happy; he's thinking about the friend's house. He looks over at his wife and says, "Is there something wrong?" She looks back at him and yells, "NOTHING!"

Is nothing really wrong with her? Of course not, she is still thinking about the fight, and she's thinking about the friend's house, and she's wondering if they should stop on the way and pick up a bottle of wine. Again, beautiful ladies, correct me if I'm wrong.

I joke but it's true. We were created to be different, but the fact still remains that we cannot allow ourselves to allow this muscle called FOCUS to get weak.

DIFFERENCE BETWEEN ACTIVITY AND ACHIEVEMENT

You may or may not know this but there is a very distinct difference between activity and achievement. One gets you something in the end while other one just keeps you busy. Knowing the difference between the two can literally mean the difference between you spending your whole life generating just enough to get by and starting to believe that chaos and feelings of anxiety are just a normal part of the process or spending less, more focused time, on specific activities that create your desired outcome. I call it focusing on your BUT or best uses of time, but I will get to that.

Take a look at your last couple of week's activities on your calendar. Have you seen a result from them or will you in the near future or are they simply put "time fillers."

STOP MULTI-TASKING!

For you to fully understand the difference between activity and achievement and stop the constant multi-tasking, we have to do one very important thing. Are you ready for this? WE HAVE TO GET OVER OURSELVES!

This was a revelation that I had in early in 2012. I was running all over the place busier than ever, and it seemed that everyone needed my attention and approval for everything. One day in particular stands out because I must have gotten four or five voicemails urging me to call back because there was an issue with this and that and just about everything else under the sun.

On that day, I decided that I was not going to call back though. I decided that I was going to wait until the end of the day and deal with everything then. At the end of the day when I called my assistant, I was surprised to hear that she didn't have that much to report to me, so I asked, "What about the issue with so and so and the others you called about?" Her response taught me so much. She simply said in a calm voice, "Oh yeah, no worries, I took care of it."

What?! I thought you needed me and the issues were world changing? Of course they were not, but she had been taught to rely on me, and when I wasn't calling back, she was forced to handle the issues she was faced with without my help from anyone else but herself.

I realized that I wasn't that important and that she could do more than I was giving her credit for and my very presence in most situations allowed her to play the role of supportive helper that didn't need to make any decisions, even though she was fully capable. Lesson learned.

Do you need to get over yourself? You may have even created a narrative in your head that you have to multi-task because you always have ten things on your to-do list and without multi-tasking, you would never be able to get them all done.

My response to you remains, "Get over yourself."

You have ten things to do at all times because you have allowed too many other people to rely on you to get things for them, to contact someone for them, to pick them up at xyz, or whatever it happens to be.

If you want to eliminate the stress that comes with multi-tasking and always having ten things to complete, you are going to have to let go of your addiction to others approval and your fear of letting other people down. Until you do this, you will continue to let yourself down and will never operate at your peak performance on a regular basis.

The truth is that we train people how to treat us. You may not like that so many people put so many demands on your time and schedule, but if you are honest with yourself, you have trained them to think that it is okay to do so.

I can remember being at an event with a Realtor and it was late at night. I think it was around 11:30. His phone rang and he looked down and saw that it was one of his clients. He ignored the call and continued to complain to me for the next five minutes about how disrespectful of his time his clients were. He told me that he had let them all know that he was going away for a few days for his convention and wouldn't be available unless it was an emergency. "How could they call me at almost midnight and think that is okay?!" he asked me angrily.

When he was all done ranting about his clients, he grabbed his phone and called his client back, who, as it turned out, just had a random question that really could have waited. The moral of the story is that as much as he complained, he still called back and acted as pleasant as ever which, in a subtle way, let his client know that calling close to midnight is perfectly okay, and if you do, you should expect a call back within five minutes.

The funny thing was that this salesperson actually had an assistant that could have handled the question the next day, but he had trained his clients to go to him for everything, no matter how big or small. This is not wise but it is common.

When my virtual coaching program first started growing by leaps and bounds, I was caught in this same trap wanting to personally respond to every question about the program and be involved in every detail, no matter how big or small. My intentions were right, but we could have never have grown to the size that we are now if I had kept that up.

Now we get a lot of questions and inquiries every day, and I never even hear about the high majority of them and that's okay because that is not the best use of my time. It might have been for a season, but all season's change and so should yours. There may be a time when you do more within your business, but you should always be trying to replace yourself. If you don't replace yourself, you will either burn out or stop growing, and when something stops growing, it is on its way toward death.

Growth isn't always measured by sales growth, but it can be evaluated by how stagnant you are. Don't allow yourself to become stagnant, either in your business or in your personal life. That's when you start to die.

To create business and not just busyness, learn to focus on two to three things a day that you want accomplish, or better yet, one thing. This is why you feel stressed out most days. You are constantly starting ten different things every morning without ever completing one thing.

In fact, there is actually no such thing as multitasking to begin with. It is really switch-tasking. You are taking your focus off one thing and moving it to another. We are actually not human capable of focusing on more than one thing at once. Think about this, and you will see just how unproductive of a practice this is in your life. Give the people around you and the projects you have chosen to focus on the attention they deserve if you want to see real results and feel fulfilled.

In the next chapter, we will talk about how to do this.

9

FOUR QUESTIONS TO ASK
EVERY MORNING

IF YOU'VE GOT to this point, then you understand the power that I believe self-talk and questions have on the way you think and act. For this reason, it is important to ask yourself the four questions that I will go over in this chapter every single morning.

I am not asking you to do anything that I myself do not do, but because of this, I can tell you with full confidence that these are the questions that will set your day up to get what it is that you want for that day and beyond.

The four questions are:

1. What
2. How
3. Why
4. Who

So let's discuss them.

WHAT?

At first glance, you probably think that the question is, "What am I going to do today?" It would make sense to train ourselves to be intentional for the day, but that is not the question that I want you to ask and I'll explain why.

The real question is, "What do I want today?" They may sound similar, but they are so completely different in the impact they can have on your day it is startling.

The problem with "What am I going to do?" is that it is an activity-focused question. The problem with activities is that they have built-in excuses for not getting the outcome that you wanted. Let me explain.

If I am having dinner later at a restaurant that I have never been to before and I am curious what's on the menu and I ask the question, "What am I going to do?" I could respond by saying to my assistant, "Could you call the restaurant and get a copy of the menu?"

Later in the day when I see my assistant, I will probably ask her if she got the menu so that I could see it, and she is going to respond, "I called the restaurant but they were busy and haven't called me back yet."

Now, did she do her job? Yes, she did. She called the restaurant but they haven't called her back yet, so technically, she did what she was asked but I did not achieve the outcome I really wanted which was to see the menu for that tonight.

This happens when you focus first on activities and not enough on what you actually want because you can fulfill activities and still never get the desired result. This is good for some people because it gives them a feeling of accomplishment that they did what they were supposed to; they just didn't get the results they desired, but it's not like they are lazy.

Some people are okay with this kind of thinking because they are not bigger-picture high achievers. They just don't want to feel like slackers, so at least, they can say they did what they set out to do even if they didn't get the result they wanted. In the end, it's not their fault, right?

But when you change the question and say "What do I want?" to start the day; everything is on the table to do what is necessary to get what you want. The answer is not limited to one particular activity; it is open to any and all activities that it takes to get the desired results. So it's not "What am I going to do?" with the answer being call the restaurant; instead, it's "What do I want?" with the answer being the menu and whatever it takes to get that menu is on the table.

The response to "What do I want?" means that my assistant can now call the restaurant, go online, drive to the restaurant, or whatever. Whatever it takes to get the menu is what she is now willing to do because her outcome is not to fulfill an activity I set for her. Her outcome is to do whatever is needed to get what she wants, which, in this case, is the menu.

Do you see the difference?

What does it mean to you in your business? Are you waking up and asking what you are going to do or are you asking what do you want? If your sole goal for a day is to sit down and make ten phone calls to potential prospects, then you can probably fulfill that activity within an hour or less. You will not be guaranteed a result, and you may or may not see a return from your time and energy spent.

On the flip side, if you woke up and asked what you wanted and the answer was that you wanted to set up an appointment with a potential new client, then all activities needed to get what you wanted are now on the table. It might take ten new calls. It might take three. It might take forty. But whatever it takes is what you are willing to do because your outcome is an actual result that you desire, not an activity that may or may not produce the result that you desire.

By the way, what you want doesn't always have to be business related at all. As I am writing this, I am getting ready for Thanksgiving and the Holiday season in general. When I wake up tomorrow on Thanksgiving, all I am going to want for that day is to spend some great quality time with my wife and children and take it all in.

Don't neglect what you want personally for what you want professionally. They do work together, and if you always prioritize your business because "you have bills to pay," you will pay the price personally which will end up affecting your business in the end anyways.

Balance doesn't always mean sharing equal time between your personal and professional life. Many times, it just means focusing on what's important at that moment. I may go to work for eight hours and only have two and a half or three hours with my kids before they go to sleep. Does that mean that I am prioritizing my career as being two to three times more important than my kids? Of course not! But when I am with my kids, I am *with* my kids. I am not hanging out on my laptop and conducting conference calls with them in the room on a regular basis because I believe my time with them is valuable and I need them to know that I am present when I am with them. Take it from a guy that speaks to large audiences on a regular basis. I can tell the ones that are present while I am speaking and the ones that are somewhere off in Florida in their mind.

Learn to be present at whatever you are doing. Just like multi-tasking is not something you should be proud of. Neither is a multi-tasking brain that can't seem to focus on what matters right in front of them. This is a struggle that most deal with but it is a battle worth fighting.

HOW?

The next question to ask your self every single morning is "How?" Now is the time that you start thinking about the actual activities that it will take to reach the desired outcome that you want. Remember though, because you now know what you want, all options are on the table for how to get there.

So what's it going to take? Will you need to do something differently than you did yesterday? Probably. How do you plan to get what you want?

The truth is that I should be able to look at your calendar and know what it is that you want for the day because math is math. Two plus two equals four, and your chosen activities should look to equal what it is that you want.

If I wake up tomorrow and have an event that I have to speak at in Orlando, then naturally, what I want for that day is to get to Orlando, and if you looked at my activities, they reflect that.

I am going to drive to the airport, board the plane, get a rental car in Orlando, and check in at the hotel. Even before that, I had to book my flight, reserve a hotel, and on and on. All of these activities assure that if I follow them, I will get what I want which is to be in Orlando when I need to be in Orlando.

But what if my connecting flight on the way to Orlando got cancelled? I guess I wouldn't make it there because, after all, I can't control if a flight will be cancelled or not, right? That is why I am still focused on what I want and not what I am going to do necessarily as my primary focus. Remember, when you focus on what you want, everything is on the table within legal bounds that will get to your desired outcome.

If my flight got cancelled, I would be looking for the next option, such as renting a car and driving the rest of the way in necessary. Believe me, I have actually done this before. I am not looking for an excuse for why something didn't work out. All I care about is getting what I want for that day regardless of what I have to do to make it happen. Some days may be easier than others, but I am focused on what I want and doing whatever it takes to get there.

Some days, it may take fewer calls than others. Some days, it may require less or more of your time. Some days may be easier than others, but the result is all that you can care about.

What do you want and what is it going to take to get it? Period.

WHY?

The third question to ask your self every morning is "Why?" Why do you do what you do? Chances are you aren't doing what you thought you would be doing when you pictured your adult life as a teenager so you chose your career for a reason. Why did you choose to do what you do?

What benefits did you associate with doing what you do everyday that may have gotten lost in your daily patterns?

The real reason that I want you to focus on your "why" every morning is because it will create the emotional endurance that is required to reach your goals. That's right—the emotional endurance.

I am well aware that most of you reading this book are more familiar with the concept of physical endurance than you are with emotional endurance but that doesn't make it any less real.

If I were to ask you to come and run ten miles with me right now and you know that you haven't run in at least five years, it would make complete sense to you that there is no way that you are going to be able to complete those ten miles with me and especially at the pace that I will probably go as a person who runs regularly. That makes complete sense, right?

Well that same principle applies to emotional endurance as well. Most of you find yourselves falling short of your outcomes all too often because you haven't developed the emotional endurance necessary to carry you through. You can't keep up the pace needed emotionally to fulfill what it is that you want to do.

That is why your "why" is so important. It reconnects you with your passion and helps to develop the emotional endurance that you are going to need to carry you through.

For example, many of you know by now that I and my two brothers were raised by a single mom. What you may not know is that I help to support a local shelter that houses and feeds single moms and their children who don't have the means to fend for themselves at the moment.

One of my "why's" has to do with the fact that I want to support this shelter and my efforts in my business help me to do that.

Your "why" can't be about money or something like that because once you become financially free, that won't push you anymore. It won't be able to create the emotional endurance you need to carry you through.

When I am exhausted and I have been in five different states or provinces in the same week and I don't want to go anywhere else, I have got to be motivated by something more than the check I will get at the next event because I may or may not need another check, and if I don't, I may just make the decision to slow down and do something else. But when I understand that if I don't get on that plane, I may not be able to donate the money needed to buy another bed at the shelter or food for the next family that needs it. I now possess the emotional endurance needed to get on the plane.

That's the power of knowing your "why" and allowing it to develop the emotional endurance needed to carry through with whatever it is that you are after.

WHO?

The fourth and final question that you must ask yourself every single morning is "Who?" Who are you going to choose to be surrounded by today?

I am not going to go into some sort of dissertation about how you need to take the five people you hang out with the most and average their incomes and it's probably right around what you make. It may or may not be true, but honestly, I don't really care.

I want you to question who you will be surrounded by today because too many of you are allowing absolute life suckers into your inner camp. You are allowing complete energy suckers to pith a tent right into your daily life, and it is slowly killing you and your goals.

I would even go as far as to say that you have people around you that don't even want you to do anything better in your life because if you did, they would feel less about themselves. They don't even realize that they feel this way, but they do.

We have already determined in chapter 1 that people are addicted to negativity, but that doesn't mean that you have to choose to be around these kinds of people because they are a barrier to the very things that you are striving so hard to achieve.

Haven't you ever met someone that just seems to always be surrounded by so much drama or so many issues? I have found that people aren't surrounded by more drama than someone else; they themselves do drama. They do problems. It's their comfort zone. Some people aren't happy or comfortable unless something bad is happening around them. How do you think that does for you and your environment?

I am well aware that this is not an easy question to ask and is even more difficult to act on, but it is necessary for the success of your business, your personal life, and the future of your family and their outlook.

Some of you are just giving way too much access and control to people that don't deserve it. Remember, nobody can drive you crazy unless you give them the keys. You wouldn't hand out a key to the front door of your house and you should be just as discerning, if not more, about those that have the keys to your soul and well-being. Why would you allow such undeserving people to have such control over your state of mind?

The answer probably lies in the fact that you never really paid this question much mind, but if I have my way, you will now begin every day with this question because it matters that much.

Most people are like garbage trucks driving around picking up everyone else's despair, anger, and depression, and when they get full, they look for someone to unload on. I have very simple advice for you: don't let it be you. Get out of that business right now.

I posted something on Facebook once that got a lot of attention, but it was so simple. I posted a quote that said, "Be the attitude that you want to be around today." So simple yet so true.

Is it easy to do? Not in the least bit. But is it worth it to try each and every day? You bet it is.

The law of attraction tells us that we attract those that are similar to us. If you don't like the types of people that you are surrounded by, do yourself a favor and look in the mirror because they are probably more like you than you realize.

This requires you to not be self-deceived so you can see yourself as you actually are. If you want to make better decisions about who you will choose to be surrounded by today, the first step is to start acting like the type of person that you would like to be surrounded by, not complaining about the type of people that seem to be attracted to you up until this point.

Start asking the right questions every morning, and you may find that you start liking the answers that you get when you are more intentional with your life.

10

FOCUS ON YOUR BUT

I HOPE YOU realize that I am not talking about diet and exercise and referring to your butt. I am talking about your best uses of time, otherwise known as your BUT.

Any psychologist will tell you that we are wired to find the negative in things way before we see the positive. That's why when you walk into a room, it seems more natural to see what is wrong with the room rather than seeing what you like about the room. You will notice it is too cold much quicker than you will notice that it is perfectly set up for what you are there for. In fact, one famous study concluded that, when it comes to the way we think, "Bad is stronger than good."

As I mentioned earlier in the book, it's really the reason why the news has a slogan, "If it bleeds, it leads." Reporters know that negativity will bring more ratings than positivity.

I mention this because this works against our level of productivity. Most of the time when we find ourselves in situations that we want to change or a business that we want to grow, we tend to ask ourselves, "What's the problem and how do I fix it?" rather than "What's working well and how do I scale it?"

That's the real power though. That's where better results come from—what's working and how do I scale it? "What's working and how do I scale it?" is the beginning to figuring out your best uses of time.

So ask your self these questions, "What do I do really well? What do I enjoy doing? What seems almost effortless like I was created to do it?" This will be the beginning of you taking your mind off of the negative and placing the focus back where it belongs—what you do well!

Your best uses of time really piggyback off of the concept I talked about previously that there is a difference between activity and achievement. One gets you something in the end while the other just keeps you busy. Figuring out your best uses of time will help you to differentiate between what is activity and what is achievement. Or in other words, what is worth your time and what is not.

There are two types of best uses of time. There are your overall best uses of time and your daily best uses of time.

Your overall best uses of time are the higher-level activities that help you to get what you want on the bigger picture scale. Meaning, if you are a real estate professional who's goal is to sell houses, then there are overall best uses of time that when repeated over and over again on a regular basis will tend to produce for you predictable and desired results on a regular basis.

HOUR OF POWER

An example of these types of best uses of time would be following through with your daily hour of power. Your hour of power is the sixty minutes that you put aside each and every workday where you shut off all distractions and focus only on activities that have the ability to bring you new revenue. It is a ritual that I believe every businessperson in every industry should be adopting because if you are not doing something daily to create business, you will eventually go out of business.

Your hour of power can include contacting past clients to stay in touch (I will discuss how to do this effectively in the next chapter), attending networking or leads groups, calling on potential new customers, or sending out marketing materials designed to make your phone ring, along with many other things. The point is to make it a part of your daily schedule that shows up on your calendar and is not optional. You don't make time to work on your business when you slow down or when you get around to it. You make the time because it is that important.

Take a moment and really think about this for a moment. If you did what I am asking you to do right now, assuming you took two weeks of vacation in the next twelve months, that would mean that you were committed to your hour of power Monday through Friday for fifty weeks in the next year. When you add that up, it means that you will spend five days a week for fifty weeks doing nothing else but focusing on activities that have the potential to bring you new business.

Do you really think that you could invest two hundred and fifty hours in the next year on these types of activities and not create new revenue? It's almost impossible when you think about it, but you have to commit to being consistent, which is where most of us lose the battle. Make the decision now to change that.

DAILY BEST USES OF TIME

After your overall best uses of time come your daily best uses of time. These are determined by how you answered the second question of your four daily questions, "How will I get what I want today?"

If you are a mortgage broker and you decided this morning that what you wanted was to create five new meaningful relationships in the real estate industry that can send you business in the future, then your best uses of time for today have to reflect this.

Your best uses of time for today might include one or all of the following:

1. Attending an event where real estate sales people will be present
2. Going through the multiple listing service and seeing who the top agents are and making contact with them by inviting them to lunch or coffee on you
3. Contacting a real estate attorney or title representative and finding out who the best and most active real estate sales people are in the area and then looking up their contact information and reaching out to them

I could go on and on but you get the point. Based on what you want for that day, you create best uses of time that have the ability to get you the outcome that you desire for that day.

TRUE BEST USES OF TIME

Keep in mind as you are reading this and starting to come up with what your best uses of time should be that I want them to be extremely specific. I don't want you to write down things like referrals, because in the end, how do you focus on referrals for your business? Do you sit down next to your phone or email and focus so hard that the phone starts to ring or messages start flying in with referrals in them? That's not possible!

Referrals are nothing more than these two things: time and circumstance. You spent enough time with someone and created enough circumstance that they trusted you enough to send you their referrals. If someone likes you, they will listen to you, but if they trust you, they will give you their business.

Be very specific with what you are going to focus on daily and make sure that they are activities that you can truly focus on.

PERSONAL GOALS SHOULD NOT BE EXCLUDED

Your best uses of time should not all be business or career related either because they are not always the best way that you should be spending your time. This is fairly obvious, but for some of you, it may not be.

For example, is it one of my best uses of time to be focusing on my hour of power on Thanksgiving or on vacation? Of course not! Why? Because what I want has changed during that time.

If I am on vacation, I have a desire to have quality time with my family and create long-lasting memories that they will carry with them for the rest of their lives. Knowing this, my best uses of time have to change as well.

On a day as such, my best use of time might be to rent a boat for the day and sail around the bay or to create sand castles with my kids.

The point is that if your best uses of time are always business or career centered, you are going to eventually burn out and desire something more fulfilling than a growing income. If you don't have people around you to share your successes with, what is the point of succeeding to begin with? Or better put, have you really even succeeded at all?

You've probably heard before, "What does it profit a man or woman if they gain the whole world but lose their soul." There are more important things than your career, but understand, I am not minimizing your career. I am just trying to get you to understand that it is a standard line for successful business people to say things like "family first," but actions speak louder than words.

Yes, there is a certain amount of sacrifice that is required for any level of success. That's what makes it worth it. But why do I continually see the family as the one that is always taking the back seat over and over again if we truly believe in "family first" like we say.

At some point, shouldn't something in your career have to take a back seat as well or see some kind of sacrifice at least?

In the past year, I took the whole summer off from travel just to be at home and hang out by the pool with my wife and kids. Even as I am writing this, I am home because I made the decision that my career as a speaker was on hold through January so I could be home during the holidays with no interruptions.

That took sacrifice. I have had to say no to companies trying to hire me during this time because it wasn't about the money; it was about the quality time with my family that is needed.

This applies to every area of your life. If you are trying to get in shape or stay in shape, then one of your best uses of time is going to include a dedicated amount of time to go to the gym and stay healthy.

I think you get the point. You need to figure out what you want from your career and your life and then create your best uses of time for that day to get whatever it is that you desire and not fall victim to your old patterns if you expect to gain anything new.

SURVIVAL OF THE FITTEST

In the same way that natural selection was conceived as a struggle for life in which only those organisms best adapted to existing conditions were able to survive and reproduce, your daily schedule should be no different.

Don't ever add something to your daily patterns without first taking something away. You should be eliminating more from your agenda than you should be adding if you want to avoid chaos and fatigue.

If your only qualifier for whether something belongs on your agenda or not is whether or not it is productive, then you are going to end up with way too many things to do than you can possibly focus on. This kind of thinking is what leads people to think that they need to multi-task in the first place.

The question is not whether an activity is productive or not. The real question is, "What are the top four activities that will get you closer to what you want for that day or week?"

This means that you are going to have to eliminate some of the patterns that you currently follow in order to focus on the higher-level activities that deserve your time.

I actually have a word for these patterns that have to go as well. They are called Not-To-Do's or NTDs.

NOT-TO-DO'S

Believe it or not, you probably can't even think of what your true NTDs are right now. If you don't believe me, think of it this way. Have you ever driven home the exact same way every single day and all of a sudden looked up and you can't even remember the last five minutes of your life? You don't even remember what happened the last five minutes! How did you turn at the last corner and not hit someone?!

You've experienced this, haven't you? Everyone has. It's what happens when we get settled into a pattern of doing things over and over again. We go into auto-pilot, but this is dangerous because it also means that we are more likely to not change the areas of our lives that need some changing. After all, if you don't know that you are doing something, how do you know to stop doing it?

To figure out what your NTDs are, I would like you to walk around for the next forty-eight hours with a pen and paper or an iPad or whatever and write down every single thing that you do during that time period. And I do mean everything! This is the only way that you will find out what you are doing that is wasting time or could be done more efficiently.

Are you checking for emails all day when you should be batching and only checking every hour or two or are you doing something else that is not productive?

One of my NTDs is that I don't answer my phone during business hours with an open-ended question like, "What's going on?" I don't do this because people have an amazing ability to turn what should be thirty-second conversations into thirty-minute conversations simply because they don't know how to get to the point or end a phone call.

It's this amazing phenomenon that when somebody calls you with a specific purpose for their call, when you say "What's going on?", they actually answer you about what is going on in their life at that moment.

The next thing you know, they are telling you about how they dropped little Johnny off at school in the morning and then stopped at the dry cleaner where they ran into Nancy and Nancy told them that... "I don't care!" That's what I really want to say. I'm trying to get things done here so what is going on? What did you call for?

To avoid this whole situation, I have learned to now answer my phone, during business hours, with the line, "Hi (insert name), I was just about to go in somewhere but didn't want to let you go to voicemail, so what's going on?"

It's amazing what happened when I started doing this. First off, they were appreciative that I didn't let them go into my voicemail, and second, they got straight to the point of why they were calling since I was about to go in somewhere.

Now, if you are going to do this, it is probably better to not have *YouTube* videos of you talking about this very point because it makes for an awkward conversation when somebody you know pretty well asks you if you are doing that thing to them that they saw you talk about on the internet. Ask me how I know that one?

So what are your top five NTDs that you need to focus on?

If you are doing it right, they should change over time and try not to compare yours to someone else's. Everyone struggles with different things, but what is important is that we recognize where we are wasting valuable time that could be spent focused on our best uses of time because time is your most valuable resource.

Most people say time is their most valuable resource, but they don't believe it. I know this because we track what we value and people track where they spend their marketing dollars. They don't track what they spend their time on and make adjustments, but they should.

I can lose money and gain it back. I can't lose time and get it back. Once it is gone, it will never be rediscovered. If you are going to value anything, learn to value how you spend your time and who you spend it with because once it is spent, it's gone for good.

11

HOW TO FINALLY GET
WHAT YOU ARE AFTER

Like most of the things I have talked about in this book, too many of us are looking at things from the wrong perspective and really working against ourselves, our goals, and our ability to get what we want.

This is no different when we our establishing what we want and how we are going to get it.

As I am writing this, I have just completed a series of Webinars with sales people to help them set up their business plans for the coming year. One of the things that always amazes me on these types of calls is how many people have no idea what their ratios are for their business and how few lines they have out there that have the potential to bring them leads.

This particular call was geared toward real estate agents, and the majority of them had on average about one to three different lines out there at any given time when they really should have fifteen to twenty.

It's common sense. If you are fishing, the more lines you have in the water, the better your chances are at catching more fish. This translates to any industry. The more lines that you have out there to generate leads, the more leads you will get and the more leads that you get, the more appointments you can set, and the more appointments that you can set, the more business you will close. It seems simple, right?

Well most things are simple, but that doesn't mean they are easy. Sometimes, it is tough for people to focus on the larger picture because they are so busy pursuing what's right in front of them and trying to master one lead generation tactic, but when it comes to lead generation, you can't think like that.

I like to put it this way: if you aren't constantly doing multiple activities designed to bring you business, then you will go out of business.

I talked about this on the business planning call I was doing and somebody put a comment that there wasn't even ten different lead-generating ideas in the whole industry that they knew of. Really?!

I responded to them by listing just a few that so many of our students utilize and then had to move on for the sake of time. The following are some of the ones I mentioned to this person:

1. SOI (Sphere of Influence)
2. Referrals from Agents
3. CORE 100 (Has the ability to create fifty to seventy sales per year if followed)

4. Geographical/Targeted Farming (Technology makes this easier and more effective than ever)
5. Open Houses (They work when done right. Like most things it's not the tool that's the issue; it's the implementation of the tool)
6. Listingstoleads/Zillow zip codes/Realtor.com zip codes/Trulia zip codes/Etc.
7. Your Website (Search Engine Optimization and Blogging)
8. Print Ads
9. Sign Calls
10. Still want to sell campaign (From my coaching)
11. Buyer Neighborhood letter (From my coaching)
12. New Listing Prospecting letter (From my coaching)
13. Rental apartments campaign (From my coaching)
14. Short Sales
15. Relocation
16. REOs/Foreclosures
17. Seminars (Offered for free to the public)
18. Pizza Order Form for all of your closings (From my coaching)
19. Hand Pick your Neighbor Campaign (From my coaching)
20. Targeted Facebook Ads

Not for nothing but that's twenty different techniques right there.

It probably isn't logical to believe that most sales people will be following all of these techniques and lead avenues all on their own, but sometimes, it does make sense to hire a virtual assistant if it is going to make you a lot more money than you are going to spend.

After all, as a sales person, aren't you really running a business? If so, then it's time to start thinking like one. There is always a cost of doing business if you are going to dominate, but the trade off can be much greater than the cost if you do it right.

If I were to say that you could get a good virtual assistant to automate your marketing for around $400/month, would you do it? Let's say that is around $5,000 for the year but that $5,000 investment brings you $100,000 in revenue, was it worth it?

The truth is that you would never stop playing that slot machine with those types of returns, but because you have never experienced the benefits, you continue to act and make decision rooted in fear.

If there is one thing that I have learned, it's that fear-based decisions rarely work out. At some point, you have to start having faith in yourself and your abilities and make the investment in yourself even when others won't.

WORKING BACKWARD

One of the best things that you can do for your business is to learn to work backward to help you figure out what you have to do to get what you want. Believe me, just staying busy enough won't get you there if you aren't busy in the direction that you need to go. If I run in the wrong direction to get to my friends house, I will still be tired. I still worked out, but I didn't get to my destination because I wasn't on the right track to get to where I wanted. Your daily activities are absolutely no different than this no matter how badly you want something.

The mistake most people make is coming up with what they want to make in the next year with no basis for how they are going to it other than, "they want it." That doesn't work.

Allow me to impress something on you. If you can't justify to me how you are going to do something other than telling me that you are a driven individual, I can just about promise you that you are about to waste a lot of energy and experience a whole lot of disappointment. There are exceptions to every rule, but you are more likely not the exception in this case.

I can vividly remember a call I had with one of my former coaching students. She was in her second year in sales, and in her first year, she had made a little over $60,000. She hired me at the beginning of her second year, and in that year, she made almost $250,000. She was ecstatic to say the least.

When I asked her what her goal was for year three, she told me it was $450,000 to which I replied, "How?"

She seemed confused and told me that after the jump she just had from year 1 to year 2, it only seemed natural. That is a huge mistake because she didn't plan on changing anything.

In order for you to grow in any real way, you have to be able to justify the growth by determining what you are going to change, adjust, or increase to justify the growth you are expecting.

When we analyzed where her business had come from the previous year, she still wasn't able to tell me why sales from a specific marketing campaign would increase this year compared to the last if she wasn't planning to expand it in some way.

I wasn't trying to be difficult but I was trying to show her that it would be difficult, if not impossible, to get what she wanted with her strategy since there was no strategy.

So the first thing you do is to figure out what kind of life do you want. Do you want to work weekends or would you rather take them off? Do you have other obligations in the evening or are you at a place in your life when you can burn the midnight oil if you need to?

These are important questions to ask because they will determine how much time you can devote to your goals and when that time can be devoted. If you are a family man with two young kids and a wife, you probably shouldn't be working through dinner with your laptop open and your cell phone near your ear on most nights. Sacrificing your family to chase after the carrot of "success" will leave you empty and wondering what you were chasing after to begin with when you realize that you have nobody there to enjoy your "success" with.

For this example, I am going to assume you are in sales of some kind. If you are not, then just make adjustments according to your industry.

Next, I want you figure out how many sales calls that you went on in the last twelve months regardless of whether you closed them or not. Let's assume for this example, it was fifty. So in the last year, you went on a total of about fifty sales calls.

Next, figure out how many sales that you closed in the last year. Let's say for the sake of this example, it was thirty-five. So you went on fifty appointments and closed thirty-five sales. That means that your closing ration is 70 percent (thirty-five closed of the fifty total appointments).

You now have the beginnings of a basis for what you need to go to the next level because you are working with something a little more tangible.

So if you did thirty-five transactions last year and you want to do fifty this year and your closing ratio remains at 70 percent, then you now know that you will have to go on seventy-two appointments because 72 × 70% = 50.4 (the total number of sales that you want).

Now that we know that you will need to go on seventy-two appointments, we now have the basis that we need to figure out what that means to you on a regular basis. Next, we need to figure out how many appointments you will have to set up on a weekly and monthly basis to make your goals happen.

To do this, you simply take the number of appointments that you are going to need for the year (in this case, seventy-two) and divide them by the number of months you plan to work in the next year (let's call it eleven) and the number of weeks you will work this year (let's call it forty-eight). This will give you the number of appointments that you will need to create each week and month to reach your goals, but it breaks down into small enough increments that it seems more possible. It's the same concept that many follow where they don't believe they could walk from here to there but they could certainly take one more step...and then one more...and then another...before you know it, you're there.

In this case, we are now going to divide seventy-two (number of appointments needed) by eleven (number of months you plan to work) which equals to 6.5 (number of appointments you need to create each month).

Then divide seventy-two (number of appointments needed) by forty-eight (number of weeks you plan to work) which equals to 1.5 (number of appointments you need to create each week).

This lets you know exactly how many appointments you need to create each week and for the month to get what you want, but it breaks them down into numbers that seem much more doable.

I do believe that you should round your numbers up though. Instead of 1.5 appointments per week, make it two appointments per week. Instead of 6.5 appointments needed per month, make it seven per month. Why? Because you are pretty much guaranteed that somebody is going to cancel an appointment on you and you don't want it to mess up your yearly goals when they do.

Now post your number somewhere that you are going to see them every work day because seventy-two appointments might seem like a steep hill to climb but is 1.5 per week that challenging if you commit to your hour of power every work day? Not when you look at it like that.

Are you telling me that if you prospected with a purpose Monday through Friday, five days a week for forty-eight weeks for a total of 240 hours, that you would not create 1.5 new appointments? Of course you would. You would actually create a lot more than 1.5 per week, but at least now, you have something to focus on.

It is also important to know what this will mean for you financially as well. To do this, take a look at what your average commission was in the last twelve months.

This is an easy thing to find out. Just look at your gross commission from last year (let's say it was $140,000) and divide it by the number of sales that you had (which was thirty-five) to get your average commission of ($140,000/35) $4,000.

Doing the math, we now know that if you do fifty transactions this year and your average gross commission was

$4,000, your gross commission this year will be ($4,000 × 50) $200,000.

The key is that you are not just saying a figure now that you want to make, but rather, you know exactly what it is going to take to get there. To make $200,000, all you will have to do is create 1.5 appointments per week. That's not so difficult, right?

It's definitely worth the effort to create 1.5 appointments per week—that's for sure.

Listen, your numbers will be different depending on where you live but you get the idea. Some of you think $200,000 is a ton of money, and others of you reading this couldn't support your family on that much money. Focus on the principle I am teaching, not the amount of money in the example.

Money is only a bi-product of your strategy, and the discipline required to consistently perform on that strategy.

ROME WASN'T BUILT IN A DAY

Another reason I am trying to get you to break down your plan in such small increments is because the overall picture can sometimes seem paralyzing, and when people feel paralyzed or unsure, they don't do anything.

By breaking your numbers down, you start to realize and focus on the fact that you don't need to make three thousand new contacts this year; you just need to make ten today, but ten today and tomorrow and every work day for the next twelve months adds up quickly, and before you know it, you have gone further than you ever thought was possible.

The last place you ever want to be in your business or life is lost, but it's an easy place to be if you don't always have an idea of what it takes to get what you want and where you are on that path.

Like being in a corn maze, it doesn't matter how close you are to an exit, if you can't see it, you are lost. Sometimes, you just need a ladder to climb up, and see just how close you really are and where you need to go to get where you are trying to get to.

That's what breaking down the numbers in your business does. It's your ladder in the corn maze of your business letting you know that although you aren't there yet, you are on your way.

I recently ran my fastest time I have ran in two years on the three-mile course that I run regularly. I had been trying to achieve this time for years and it felt amazing!

Then one week later, I ran the same course and I ended with a time over a minute slower than what I had just done the week before.

I wasn't surprised though. I didn't feel like running that day and had zero motivation to get my running clothes on and run in the cold. It taught me a couple of things though.

First, it taught me that you aren't always going to be at your peak performance, but when you understand the smaller steps that have to be taken every day to reach your goal, you do them anyway.

I had a goal to run over five hundred miles this year, and the idea of even driving five hundred miles drives me insane so the thought of running that far—you can only imagine. But I didn't have to run five hundred miles. I only had to run three miles today. It's that simple. Whether I felt like it or not, whether I could do it as fast as usual or not, my job was to run three miles today.

So I put my running clothes on and told my wife that I was going running. I still wasn't sure that I was, but I thought by telling my wife that I was I would now have to. That's an accountability partner in action.

The second thing that this experience taught me was the power of breaking goals down into smaller increments. I knew that the next time I went out, since I was off on this day, I would not only want to beat today's time but also the time that I set the week before that was my fastest time in two years.

To do this, I would have to run about ninety seconds faster than I did on this day. That seemed particularly daunting. Ninety seconds is a long time to make up over a three-mile period, so I couldn't really wrap my mind around it.

So instead, I asked myself if I could shave thirty seconds per mile. That seemed doable. And yet it was still ninety seconds, but when broken down, it seemed a little more achievable.

This works in so many areas of your life. I am going to fly over 150,000 miles in the air this year, and I'm not really looking forward to it. In fact, it doesn't even sound feasible.

But you know what I can do? I can get on my flight to Dallas on Thursday and back to New York on Saturday. You see how this works? I couldn't fathom flying this much, but I can fathom getting on my next flight.

Don't let large goals or numbers create mental blocks for you that paralyze you and force you into inaction. Break everything down to the smaller, more realistic interval and go after that.

Again, you probably can't imagine making three thousand new contacts this year, but can you do ten today? Yes, you can!

THE NEED FOR COMFORT
AND CERTAINTY

The truth is that making money is not difficult—it's different. When most of us think about being different, we picture being crazy or weird and thinking outside of the box, and yet to really be different in this world, all it really takes is to be consistent. Unfortunately, it has become the norm to be constantly doing and trying new things whether they work or not.

I think people do this so that they have something to blame if they don't do well. If you are constantly doing something different, then you can reason that you aren't doing well because the last thing didn't work but now you are trying something new, right?

As I have said over and over again, for most people, the issue is not that they don't know what to do; it's simply that they don't do it!

It's human nature to want to do what is comfortable and stay away from what is uncomfortable. If I were to try to poke you in the eye, what are you going to naturally do without even thinking about it? You are going to close your eye and try to stop me, right?

It's the reason why some of us are more motivated in our fitness life than we are in our career or vice versa. We are comfortable in the gym. We know what we are doing and we feel like we've seen pretty good results, but when it comes to our career, we are not as comfortable because we don't feel like we are solely responsible.

One of the six basic human needs is something called certainty. The amount of certainty we feel in many situations ultimately determines how we act or don't act.

In the case of the gym, if you put in the work, you are fairly certain that you will get the results that you desire, but in your career, you may not feel as certain because you could step out and call someone only to hear them say "no." That can be very scary for some of you, but do you know what is even scarier to me? Not doing well enough in my career to be able to afford that gym membership. I am fairly "certain" that if I don't do what I need to in my career, then I will not be able to attend my gym anymore.

This makes the point that you can alter the certainty that you feel based on the meaning that you assign to the activity in front of you.

BEST-CASE/WORST-CASE

That's why I believe so much in the best-case/worst-case method. It's pretty simple, and I actually got to demonstrate it on a recent coaching broadcast that I did with all of our students watching live.

It applies to just about anything though. You can use it for business or personal for just about anything that you know you should do but just aren't following through with.

It goes something like this.

In the case of my student, she was having an issue with the prospecting that she needed to do within her business. The idea of picking up the phone and reaching out to someone she didn't know or knocking on the door of someone that wasn't expecting her scared her mightily.

It didn't matter how good her scripts were or how targeted the people were she was supposed to contact. She just wasn't comfortable with it because her certainty gauge wasn't very high.

So I told her take out a blank piece of printer paper and write at top left hand side "Best-Case" and on the top right hand side "Worst-Case." Then I told her to draw a line down the center of the paper.

I then said to her, "If you did do what makes you uncomfortable and prospected to people you didn't know, what is the worst-case scenario? What is the absolute worst thing that could happen as a result?"

She thought about it for a second, and then she said, "Well… they might reject me. They could say 'no,' or they could even be upset at me for bothering them for contacting them when they didn't ask me to."

All valid points.

I told her to write down everything that she had just said to me on the right hand side of her paper under the worst-case column in big letters and she did.

I then asked her, "If you did do what makes you uncomfortable and prospected to people you didn't know, what is the best-case scenario? What is the absolute best thing that could happen as a result?"

She thought about it for a second, and then she said, "Well…I might make a sale worth $8,000. I could pay off my student loans and start to travel without worrying about money. I could be financially free."

When she was done, I told her to write down everything that she had just said to me on the left hand side of her paper under the best-case column in big letters and she did.

I then asked her to hold up the paper and just look at it for a moment and picture her life under each scenario. I told her to really go there, picture it and what it feels like living life on both sides of the paper.

After she had done this for a little bit, I asked her what it was like on the right hand side, the worst-case scenario side. How has your life changed as a result?

She said under the worst-case scenario, her life wouldn't really be any different. Basically by not doing what I wanted, nothing was going to change. Nothing that terrible was going to happen to her, and by not acting, she was actually guaranteeing the exact same result that she feared so much in her worst-case scenario—they would say no.

Having no results at all left her in the exact same position that people saying "no" would have anyway.

Interesting…

So I said, "What about the left hand side? What was it like picturing life in the best-case scenario?"

She said it was amazing and that she would be so much better off in her life and finally feel financially free and "comfortable" for the first time ever.

Isn't that also interesting?

All I really did was refocus her on the comfort she could feel by doing what was uncomfortable which connected her to her basic human need for certainty because to not act would mean that she would "certainly" not get what she wanted out of life. She had just never had it so plainly defined for her in a way that made sense.

Her example is like so many others in that the very things that we fear never happen. The majority of the things we worry about never happen. When you worry, you suffer twice; once when you worry and again if the thing you are worrying about ever actually happens.

More importantly though, by choosing not to act on whatever your thing is, you essentially guarantee that you will live on a daily basis in your worst-case scenario without ever doing anything that has the power to enable you to live in your best-case scenario.

Make a decision right now to live on the left side of the paper no matter what it takes.

12

FINAL WORDS

I NEVER WOULD have imagined as a young kid without a father figure that one day, I would get the opportunity to father two incredible boys. I never would have imagined that thousands of people would actually pay to gain access to my content in my programs. I never would have imagined that a kid, who was constantly told to be quiet (putting it nicely), would one day actually get paid to talk. I never would have imagined that I, who am pretty introverted by nature, would one day have thousands of people that follow me and engage daily.

I never "would" have imagined, but at some point, I had to change that and start imagining. You really won't do anything that you can't imagine in your mind.

I remember hearing one time that if your dreams are something that you can accomplish on your own, then they aren't big enough and you really don't need God at all. Your dreams have to be so big that you can't take credit when you achieve them.

That, in a nutshell, is how I feel.

When you look at some of the people that have supported me and promoted my content, it might not have made any sense at the time. Frankly, it didn't make sense to me either, but I continued to work hard, hustle, and make sure that I was ready whenever called upon.

I wasn't always where I needed to be, but I was always on my way. I made mistakes, but I learned from them and allowed them to make me a better husband, father, speaker, coach, and entrepreneur.

I decided to take what others discounted as "clichés" and turn them into belief systems that I followed.

Clichés like, "What others put in your way to become a stumbling block, choose instead to use as a stepping stone to the higher calling you are after."

I believe that and I try every day to live it.

To me, these are more than just mere words. They are empowering insights into universal truths that I can choose to believe and act on or I can toss them to the side and ignore them and continue to operate in my current complacency and limiting self-narrative.

I get emails and messages all the time from people that give me credit for changing their life in some way or another, and in every case, I tell them the same thing. I didn't change anything. YOU changed your life. YOU changed your business. I said the same thing to you that I have said to thousands of others, but YOU decided to act on what you heard and started to imagine a different story for yourself and took action to back it up.

The same is true with this book. Some of you will read it, get motivated, and then read ten more books making you feel the same way without ever doing anything that results in change for your life or business. That is not my hope for you.

Others though will read this book and look for areas of your life and business that you can change, no matter how difficult it seems, and actually act.

That is my hope for you.

Zig Ziglar once said, "You can get everything in life that you want if you will just help enough other people get what they want."

That is the giving spirit that we all need to aspire to.

I ask you this one thing. If this book has helped or inspired you at all, then buy a copy for someone else that needs it as well.

I hope that I get the opportunity to connect with you and meet you in person one day. Our world seems more connected than ever before so let's keep that going!

Remember that your life is a book and you hold the pen. Make sure you write a story worth reading.

God bless you.